VISIONARY
LEADERSHIP

How Association Leaders Embrace
Disruption in the 21st Century

SETH KAHAN

Complete this short assessment to find out

STRONGLY
DISAGREE   1 —— 2 —— 3 —— 4 —— 5   STRONGLY
AGREE

I. Personal Power

I make it a priority to...

____ Purposefully do things I have never done before to add to my experience

____ Use stories to get and hold people's attention on important topics

____ Regularly make time for activities that renew and revitalize me

____ Find innovative ways to package experience into stories that illustrate key lessons

____ Ask members and staff about their life experience

____ Listen for stories from members that hold valuable lessons

____ Put myself in the shoes of people I don't agree with

____ Guard my time that is scheduled for taking care of myself

____ ADD THE NUMBERS ABOVE FOR YOUR TOTAL SCORE ON PERSONAL POWER

II. Association Leadership

I make it a priority to...

____ Maintain an attitude of opportunism when circumstances are challenging

____ Reach out to other parts of the organization to get insight

____ Help others learn and grow in the face of adversity

____ Find the silver lining in every major problem I encounter

____ Find ways to join forces with other organizations to achieve our shared goals

____ Bring together multiple constituencies to address difficult issues

New competencies in three categories—*Personal Power, Association Leadership, and Market Acumen*—prepare you for more effective collaboration with and influence on the systems in which you operate. I have developed this assessment to help you determine the areas that would most benefit your personal and professional growth.

____ Excel at building partnerships across multiple organizations

____ Find alignment among parties who represent differing perspectives

____ ADD THE NUMBERS ABOVE FOR YOUR TOTAL SCORE ON ASSOCIATION LEADERSHIP

III. Market Acumen

I make it a priority to...

____ Read outside our association to understand how the world is changing.

____ Identify market changes that could have major impact on my association

____ Hunt for social trends that could threaten my association

____ Determine the disruptions that are likely to last

____ Educate myself on complicated trends

____ Dig deep and probe into new advances that impact our work

____ Contact our members and learn what is changing in their day-to-day work

____ Shift organizational priorities with the market, not waiting for periodic strategic planning

____ ADD THE NUMBERS ABOVE FOR YOUR TOTAL SCORE ON MARKET ACUMEN

These leadership competencies are the subject of Chapter 2. To see my recommendations based on your self-assessment as a Visionary Leader, turn to page 42.

ISBN: 0-9759206-2-6

Printed in the United States of America.

This book and others by Seth Kahan are available at special quantity discounts.
Contact: Seth@VisionaryLeadership.com • VisionaryLeadership.com/thebook

Contents

*I dedicate this book to all association leaders
who want to use their position to make great contributions to society
in line with their organization's mission.*

*Here's to your success.
The world needs your members' expertise and experience.
You are in a unique position to help them deliver.*

*Getting Change Right:
How Leaders Transform Organizations from the Inside Out*

*Getting Innovation Right:
How Leaders Leverage Inflection Points to Drive Success*

*Building Beehives:
A Handbook for Creating Communities that Generate Returns*

FOREWORD

C. David Gammel, FASAE, CAE
Executive Director
Entomological Society of America

In 2014 Seth and I watched 1.5 million bats stream from under the Congress Avenue Bridge into the late summer evening sky of Austin. The migratory bats that make their home under the bridge for part of the year will consume up to 20,000 pounds of insects a night. It is a profound sight to see and an amazing demonstration of nature in action. It was the perfect setting for the work we did the following day with the leadership community of the Entomological Society of America. That session, where we explored grand challenges and the role of entomology to solve them, set the stage for significant growth and impact of this 130-year-old membership society representing a mature discipline. Coming out of that event, our rallying vision was to position the Society as a key platform for engaging with the biggest challenges facing humanity on a global basis to which entomology can and must make a significant contribution.

That vision subtly and profoundly changed everything and unlocked significant growth across our programs. Seth opened that door for us.

I've known Seth for many years now, as a friend, mentor, and thought partner. We share the belief that our organizations can serve a unique and powerful role in society. Associations, at their best, change lives and the world for the better. He is passionate about the potential of associations and I've seen his eyes light up with excitement over meals or drinks talking about the possibilities and how to make them a reality. His enthusiasm on this topic is infectious and delightful.

We also both believe that associations must change to achieve that potential. With the myriad options available to people and organizations today, simple operational excellence is not enough to create a thriving organization with impact. We have to lift our eyes and chart a course over the horizon. This is Seth's forté. The book in your hand or on your screen sums up so much of his best thinking on transformation for associations.

I called Seth one day and complained about being overwhelmed with tasks and minutia to the point I was locked up, making no progress on anything. His advice: Identify the single most important thing you can do today and do it. It cut right through my mental clutter and unlocked a path forward. I still use that almost daily. This entire book is like that advice: practical, powerful, doable, and it will deliver results.

As Seth points out so eloquently in these pages, transformation is not an interruption of our work, it is the work.

Embrace it!

INTRODUCTION

The Old Paradigm

A group of professionals threw their money in a pot to get things done together they couldn't do alone—lobbying, identifying and sharing best practices for success, education, a magazine with the latest news, and so on. They needed a way to govern and bylaws were established. They set it up so those who'd been around the longest, who had accrued the greatest degree of knowledge and wisdom, became the board of directors. To prevent power from accumulating in a small group of members, they created a revolving door for leadership. When getting things done turned out to be consistently more effort than the board of directors had the time or inclination to carry out, they hired an executive director, and when, eventually, that individual couldn't do it all, a staff was brought on.

Together, the executive director and staff were the executive arm. They didn't plan or strategize, though they could convene those who did. As matters grew more complicated, as market conditions changed and the environment became more complex, the executive director was given greater power to strategize.

This seems a fairly simple outline of organizational growth—as the demands of the organization grow, its leaders rearrange design and strategy to meet its burgeoning needs. But what if there's another way to look at it, a different perspective that makes it easier to see the next stage?

The New Paradigm

What if an organization is in fact a more highly complex, organic structure, with its own collective intelligence, its own life path, and even its own capacity to acquire greater strength and purpose? Just as atoms become molecules become cells become organs become creatures, can humans, when organized together, become a greater body inside a well-functioning organization?

Consider biological evolution: At some point in Earth's history, single-celled life elegantly, exponentially exploded—quite the disruptive innovation—into multicellular forms. Then came more organized invertebrates, then vertebrates, then fishes, which soon crawled right out of the sea. Eventually, reptiles and mammals emerged, and finally, once upright, *homo sapiens* walked the Earth. It was a slow start by our standards, but we were off and running, hunting and gathering and spreading to the four winds, then forging tools and plowing fields and forming militaries, laws, and city-states. We began conquering and colonizing, exploring and warring, and otherwise making terrible messes and beautiful art. Eventually, planes and trains, atom bombs and automobiles, and soon enough, we'd covered the planet, documented scientific advancement, generated industry, developed professions, and built interconnected markets and societies with international reach. Then came the digital revolution and in a matter of years we were literally one planet, and every single person had the ability to communicate to any other earthling in real time. This, of course, delivered a corresponding revolution in the ways organizations operate and grow.

We are becoming a new kind of species—connected as never before, and with the power to not only imagine the future but see clearly many possible outcomes and to influence through our efforts which ones come to pass.

It was a French paleontologist, geologist, and Jesuit priest who once said, "Evolution is a light illuminating all facts, a curve that all lines must follow." Pierre Teilhard de Chardin was a radical visionary born before his time who understood something fundamental about all systems: they evolve; they transcend themselves.

What is it that makes humans unique among all the Earth's creatures? We transform ourselves. We imagine what is possible and then create it or *become* it.

The very nature of evolution is transformative *disruption*.

The word *disruption* has come to have a new meaning: jarring jumps that puncture previous limits, establishing new capabilities and pushing boundaries in dramatic moves. When one of these jumps changes the game, making possible something that did not exist before, it's a disruptive innovation. This is the kind of disruption I am referring to here. It's important to understand this dynamic because it is now making inroads into every aspect of our lives, personal and professional.

Leaders are now accelerating change intentionally, strategically. We are leveraging technology to extend trust and therefore our reach. We are becoming skilled at both predicting and influencing the future. Referring to his theory of disruptive innovation, scholar and author of *The Innovator's Dilemma*, Clayton Christensen, discusses its visionary capacity. Since there is no available data about the future, the only way to predict future outcomes reasonably is with a good theory, he explains. "By teaching managers to look into the lens of theory [of disruption] into the future, you can actually see the future very clearly."[1]

Now, use your imagination and follow me into a strange world where organizations and technology are the living extensions of humanity. Imagine for a moment that organizational growth works just like human development. After fertilization (the idea and commitment to begin a new association), among the first tissues of the fetus to form are the brain and nervous system (the Board of Directors, executive director, and staff). From there, all other tissues and organs develop with the central organizing facility relayed through these systems (committees form, communication tools to disseminate knowledge are created, and conferences take place). As this body develops, it is always an organized whole at every stage of development, but progressively becomes more complex (the association grows and the industry or profession thrives from the activity of members).

As with individuals, associations grow more cohesive and intelligent as they begin to interact more skillfully with their environment. With greater complexity, this living system begins to move out into the world with deeper penetration, no longer confined to a single body but showing up in multiple facets of society (the growth of individual trades and professions is less insular and more interdependent with other trades and professions). And society isn't inert or passively receptive. It develops and evolves, too, creating connections wherever greater value is to be had—so the change becomes exponential (where associations partner and collaborate with major social systems, they prosper and ride growth to greater impact, collecting more resources to fuel this growth). The demands on the organization's structure grow more complex, and its need to develop still further—in totally new ways—is required.

Considering today's social environment—from global social media destinations to the rapid proliferation of affordable apps—we see professionals finding new ways to interact and create value outside of associations. Whether or not they are acknowledged as formal members, they nonetheless play in the space and often create valuable results. This dissipates the value of traditional associations.

Regardless of the traditional standard of membership, emerging professionals benefit from new opportunities in society, such as the democratization of knowledge, for example, through free training provided by many top universities via the Internet. No longer constrained by formal recognition, entrepreneurs are flooding into spaces once guarded carefully. For example, in the recent Xprize awarded for cleaning up oil spills, the competitors included a retired police inspector, a tattoo artist, and a former pro basketball player. The solution that emerged outperformed what the oil industry, with all its engineers and technicians had been able to develop—by a factor of three!

This is happening because technology is now ubiquitous and cheap, and therefore, so is communication. We can connect with anyone today, whenever and wherever they may be, easily exchanging information and learning from one another. Social class and other institutional barriers are much more permeable than they have ever been.

Will this evolutionary disruption make

associations into dinosaurs, or will their leaders discover a stronghold of unrealized value? If they choose simply to clean out the attic, selling off whatever valuables are found up there and throwing the rest away (let's keep the conference, but throw away the magazine), associations will go the way of the dinosaur. But if they challenge themselves to peer into their own unrealized evolutionary potential and engage with, and *as*, new forms, they'll survive and help create that future.

Professional associations have a long history. The renowned religious order of scholars and teachers known as the Jesuits (Teilhard de Chardin's sacred order) was founded in sixteenth-century Spain and can be likened to a professional association. Indeed, scientific and professional societies are believed to have existed for centuries—and may well exist for many more. Whether or not associations survive the oncoming technological and social disruptions of the modern marketplace will depend on the visionary capacity of their leaders. This includes a willingness to embrace change for the good of larger society (less insular and self serving in their missions), as well as the ability to discern between the true gifts of associations (saving and improving on them for future generations) and those relics of either leadership or organizational function that have outlived their time.

We stand at the precipice of a radically new future. Many longstanding associations will perish. For every leader unwilling to take the leap, there will be a dozen opportunists sending in drone helicopters, throwing lifelines to your savviest professionals. They will parlay *your* work into their growth.

But if you're willing to explore new kinds of listening, organizing, and executing so that you are future-oriented, with visionary leadership at your core, then when you step out over the edge, you just may be able to fly.

A Visionary Leader

SUSAN NEELY

When Susan Neely, now president and CEO of the American Council of Life Insurers, began her previous tenure as president and CEO of the American Beverage Association (ABA) in May 2005, it was a time of tremendous tension around the sale of soft drinks and sugar-sweetened beverages in American schools. When Neely joined the ABA, legislation was being pursued at the state level that would place restrictions on the sale of these beverages to children in school environments.

Neely wisely recognized that her organization had a critical role to play. Some influential groups were arguing for an outright ban against the sale of soft drinks and sweetened beverages in schools, but rather than stand in opposition to these restrictions, Neely believed the American Beverage Association should take a forward-leaning position. Under her leadership, she guided the ABA to ask not what was merely in their own best interest, but...

what was the right thing to do?

Neely believed the answer to this question would lie with parents—especially with moms, who tend to be the gatekeepers to what their families consume.

> *"If your associations' members are some of the most valued consumer product companies in the world,"* says Neely, *"they didn't get that way without listening to their consumers. So, for us, it was critical to ask parents, 'What beverages do you think should be available to your children when they are in school, and how can we as an industry support you?'"*

The answer from parents wasn't what some activists would have wanted (i.e., that no one should ever have a Coca-Cola, Pepsi, or Dr Pepper in their lives). Instead, positions were overwhelmingly more nuanced. "Parents were saying, 'Sure, our kids can have soft drinks. We just want some guidelines, particularly for our young children, around what they have access to when we're not with them. We'd like there to be more controls.' It's really that simple. That led us to a policy that provided appropriate choices for elementary, middle and high schools."

It turned out that for younger children (those below high school age), parents wanted limited options, such as low-fat milk, 100 percent juice, and water. But for those in high school, a typical parent's response was like this one: "I'd be happy if my biggest concern was that my teen wanted to drink a Coke or Pepsi, but I'm concerned about many more things than that."

In this way, the notion of soft drink intake as a major crisis was debunked. For teenagers, primary parental concerns turned out to be a focus on caloric intake, providing students the ability to make informed choices, and limiting those choices to only lower-calorie and/or smaller-portion options.

From commitment to credibility: Legislative (and presidential) buy-in

With consumer input in hand and their chief aim in mind—to do what was *right*—the ABA made a bold voluntary commitment: to shift the product mix of beverages sold in schools.

Their news caught the attention of former President Bill Clinton. He contacted the ABA regarding a new entity he was putting together, the Alliance for a Healthier Generation, which would focus on healthier schools. Clinton found the ABA announcement intriguing and was interested in working together.

In order to enter into a formal partnership with the Alliance for a Healthier Generation, founded by the American Heart Association and the William J. Clinton Foundation, the ABA had to commit to remove full-calorie soft drinks from schools within a specific timeframe—just three school years. They had to also agree to have their program audited by an independent evaluator and to provide public progress reports. About the experience, Neely says, "We now had some of the most valued trademarks in the world on board. Failure was not an option."

It's important to note that Neely had committed to doing the right thing *before* getting industry and membership buy-in. She committed to align with both her members' and the children's best interest. This is a solid demonstration of visionary leadership.

Inventing a new paradigm:
Industry buy-in

The ABA's formal announcement came in a press conference in May 2006 and was well received by the public health community, including mainstream policymakers and others interested in contributing to society through their work. Neely reflects, "It was an interesting new paradigm, for an NGO (non-governmental organization) and a major sector of the American economy to partner together. And it created a new set of responsibilities and challenges for the ABA, because we don't put anything in a bottle or contract to sell products with schools. We needed to understand how to help these ferocious competitors come together to deliver on the commitment we had all made."

The collective agreement of the membership of an association does not automatically translate into action by the individual players. It requires a Herculean effort to secure that action, especially among competitors. Neely and the ABA were up to the task.

One aspect of the ABA's role was to champion the cause and communicate on a massive scale, beginning with the major beverage manufacturers—Coke, Pepsi, and Dr Pepper—who have the lion's share of the market and distribute through a whole system of independent bottlers. The bottlers (also members of

the ABA) could choose not to participate, so it became the role of each manufacturer to communicate to its bottlers and distributors, with the ABA as "additional surround sound," on why the effort was ultimately good for business.

The ABA also brought in an ombudsman, a deputy general counsel who helped alleviate any competitive concerns—for example, that one competitor was honoring the agreement and another was not. The agreement was that the beverage manufacturers would no longer sell full-calorie soft drinks in schools. And in high schools where students had more options, these beverages would be capped at 100 calories per 12-ounces and be made available in the smaller portion sizes.

This was sweeping change! And like all change, it wasn't without challenges.

Vending machines weren't set up to vend the smaller-portion beverages in 12-ounce containers. They had to be retrofitted for the new package size; these new package sizes had to be created; the new products needed to be formulated; and contracts rewritten to address the new commitment—and, again, all within three years. The beverage companies had to train their marketing and sales teams about the new portfolio and why the effort was underway. Sales and marketing materials needed revising.

"This was a multi-million-dollar implementation, paid for by the companies themselves," says Neely. "At ABA, it was our work to oversee that everyone honored their voluntary commitment."

By year three, the ABA and the major beverage companies had achieved a remarkable 88 percent reduction in beverage calories shipped to schools. A paid external advertising campaign ensued, to demonstrate to members and the public that the industry had delivered on its commitment to change the school beverage landscape.

In their later work with Michelle Obama, they agreed to put a standardized, uniform calorie label on the front of every can, bottle, and pack. Asking the beverage manufacturers to give up valuable real estate on their product labels was a monumental ask, but they succeeded.

The credibility that comes from competitors working together

The traditional corporation model is largely self-preserving and protective. Companies simply don't go out of their way to work with their competitors. But the school beverage effort proved that even fierce corporate competitors can put rivalry aside to work together on a worthy effort, and through their collaboration, acquire greater esteem and public goodwill.

"Everyone is familiar with the 'cola wars,'" says Neely. "So, when the public saw these three global trademarks volunteering to work on this together, there was instantaneous credibility." And this is an achievement Neely is particularly proud of—bringing together major competitors to create a massive industry shift and positively impact the lives of thousands of kids and families for years to come.

The CEO as tuning fork for the organization

When Susan looked out at the cultural indicators, she could clearly see change on the wind. Collectively, we were shifting toward greater concern for health and fitness, including a desire for awareness of the ingredients in our consumables. Neely knew this would have an impact in the beverage industry, one way or another.

Since the National School Beverage Guidelines initiative altered an entire industry, Neely observes three central areas of growth in her own leadership: conviction, credibility, and contribution. What had been for Neely a gut instinct in the beginning—to consider not simply what was in the organization's best interests, but what was right—is now a firm conviction, intensified and multiplied many times over based on her experiences. Through this effort she established credibility, taking on a seemingly intractable challenge and succeeding with flying colors. Contribution is now a hallmark of her leadership. "I now know that what is right for the organization to do," she says, "is *essential* to success."

To look ahead and see clearly that right path requires strategic foresight. Neely saw something that others didn't see at first. She knew there was something the ABA needed to get in front of, to take a forward position on. This stance did no less than transform the way an entire industry manufactures, bottles, and distributes beverages to our schools.

"Invariably," says Neely, "issues ripen. People can't always see what the CEO sees, but they're going to see it eventually."

chance

change

opportunity

innovation

strategy

Be a Jedi at facilitating leadership in others.
Simultaneously address the profound and the mundane.
Train yourself to be a midwife of the future.
Recognize greatest limitations are mental states.
Embrace self-transformation.

One

VISIONARY LEADERSHIP

"I must be willing to give up what I am in order to become what I will be."

—Albert Einstein

When I met Susan Neely in her office, she told me, "I have a strong belief in the power of associations because inherent in them is the power of collective action—the power of different sectors of the American economy to do *good*." She was named 2017's Trade Association CEO of the Year. And rightly so; she's emblematic of today's visionary leader.

"Trade associations are predicated around a healthy focus on policy and advocacy," Neely explains, "as well as for advancing specific policies that support their representative sector aims. But American associations can no longer be successful without identifying and seriously committing to what we are *for*."

Here she contrasts a reactive position, where many trade associations define themselves by what they are against. While they have internal aspirations that their board endorses, to the outside world they seem only to rise up when their interests are threatened. They seem not to stand for positive change. Neely reverses that perception and claims the rewards that go with it.

The need to commit to strong *for*-positions, she says, "... is magnified many times when your members own some of the most valued trademarks in the world—important companies, global in their scope. Such companies recognize the need to actively engage with their consumers and their communities, as well as to publicly stand on the side of making a positive social contribution," not merely representing *against* positions in their space.

Neely rightly emphasizes a critical new insight for association leaders as they think about organizational strategy, one she strongly believes they'll be less effective without. "In the old days of the last century, associations could simply identify a set of principles or values they sought to represent, and that would be enough." While those are important...

Today's leaders must go farther than espousing their **core values;**
• • •

THEY
MUST
ACTIVELY
EMBODY
THEM.

Visionary leadership is transformative. Once inspired, it penetrates the ordinary; it reaches through time to bring out the very best the world has to offer. A visionary leader not only anticipates events, but *actively influences* the future. Visionary capacities are infectious; nurturing your own enables others to flourish in fundamental ways.

In associations, visionary leadership identifies challenges and growth opportunities *before* they happen, while positioning the organization to produce extraordinary results that make a genuine contribution to members and to the world. Yet, most of the visionary leaders I know wouldn't use this moniker for themselves; they're simply doing their jobs the way they know how. So, what is it visionaries do that others don't?

They're masters at analyzing the environment, scanning for untapped capabilities, examining their members' unmet needs, mining core expertise, and sensing future potentialities. They're adept at detecting larger patterns and predicting possibilities for collective impact. They spot new VIPs from whom to learn, as well as key partners with whom to engage—in substantive visioning; bringing together emerging trends and insights; and giving shape to what is possible in the near-term. Visionary leaders are good at leaning in and listening. They're Jedis at facilitating leadership in others; true craftspeople at capturing chance, change, and opportunity; and the first in line to seize the right innovative strategy.

Visionary leaders are midwives of the future.

They are masters at zeroing in on all that is required to succeed, holding those aims steady and strong, communicating and defending the possibilities they see to any audience. They mine these strengths to bring into existence rich seeds of potential value until those seeds grow into actual value. They're opportunistic, exploiting chances offered by immediate circumstances.

They move fast to secure ground and bring along their board and other key influencers in order to take advantage of openings.

They are masters at simultaneously addressing the profound and the mundane. They know how to lead and coach their constituency to recognize and embrace opportunity in the context of their industry or profession's day-to-day needs.

Visionaries cultivate the *mind field*—a collective spirit and sense of capability—among their most important players: their chair and board, influential members, key partners, senior management team, and the rising stars inside their organization. They recognize that peoples' greatest limitations are their mental states, which determine what they believe is possible and how well they perform. So, visionaries build a strong sense of collective ability and individual commitment.

While they may participate in periodic strategic planning exercises, visionary leaders never cease thinking strategically and expect the same from their most powerful allies, inside and outside the organization. And they use *real-time strategy*, a visionary competency emerging to meet a world accelerating in both capabilities and disruptions.

Visionary leaders embrace self-transformation. They know their current capabilities are a reflection of their internal models, which spring directly from their personal experiences and beliefs. As a result, they set out to change themselves in order to become clearer minded and more influential, developing deeper understanding and broader application as they go. They're leaders who recognize that their minds are their ultimate instruments, so they're relentless about self-development. It is far more effective to lead through modeling transformation than preaching it.

Visionaries do all of this because it's their job to continuously foster new value—not just by creating increases in existing value (think better and higher quality for existing offerings), but to engender game-changing value that comes from the sidelines and is almost impossible to generate (like apps identified by members that provide unmet needs, or seemingly wild-eyed initiatives that serve new populations outside of the current frame of reference).

While working on a strategic plan in the printing equipment industry in 2010, I had the good fortune to talk with the head of Americas Graphics Solutions Business Imaging and Printing Group for what was at the time the third largest publicly held company in the United States. We were discussing growth in a contracted market, just following the mortgage crisis in America and the same year that Apple sold 14 million iPads in ten months, changing the print industry forever.

During our conversation, it felt to me as if he were standing on the prow of a great ship and it wasn't enough for him that he was positioned at the prow. He was up on the railing leaning as far out as he could to see an extra three feet. He was so excited about the future, even though that future was taking his world apart.

He told me that his organization had customarily done strategic planning every three years. Then every year. But soon, he realized he could only hire managers and leaders who did strategy in real time. He shared how every one of his managers was in the field learning about their customers' needs in a world that simply wasn't slowing down. They needed to spot opportunities for growth which had to be acted on quickly, and this changed the future of the organization. He wanted them to be able to identify overarching interests for his company; the

means of achieving them; and the decisions required to capture opportunity. He expected managers to act on their insights and bring them back so the mother organization could integrate new direction in real time, not waiting for periodic review.

By way of example, he shared how the mortgage crisis of 2009 had turned his customers upside down—the national economic contraction reduced customer demand precipitously—and how he used this very disruption to grow a new line of business worth over a billion dollars. The organization had been like a great ocean liner, he told me; it couldn't make sharp turns. He knew his organization wasn't nimble enough to check out every new development on the horizon, so he maintained what he called a *fleet mentality*. He partnered with many smaller organizations that were nimble and could investigate disruptions. In return, his enterprise allowed them to ride in its wake, protecting them from massive upsets to the market, such as the mortgage crisis.

How to Turn Turmoil to Advantage

Innovating in a disruptive environment means taking adverse conditions and finding ways to use their force to your advantage. Like an expert sailor, you can use any wind direction to make progress. Disruption is the wind. It may blow against you, but properly harnessed, it will take you where you want to go.

To illustrate, let's assume your customers are facing a major set of challenges, causing them severe anxiety with their own businesses. This could be due to a market turn, a contracting economy, or a new player that is changing their game. Whatever the disrupting factor, you can use it to your advantage by addressing your customers' most pressing concerns.

When the crisis hit, so many of their customers were impacted that he made the decision to extend to them their own Customer Relationship Management software (CRM), an excellent tool. Doing so helped many survive the assault on their business and increased their effectiveness. This decision worked so well that soon, their customers began to ask if they could provide the CRM to their own customer base. Doing so quickly became an enormous advantage, connecting them to *two* tiers of business customers, giving them access to trends and needs across the industry.

Soon, the CRM was providing a significant revenue stream that complemented his graphics business and generated substantial profits. This was how real-time strategy guided him to a game-changing innovation that served the world of graphics.

In the chapters ahead, I will outline further visionary leadership competencies and describe their interplay with strategy as it operates in our current age of disruption.

Consider these examples:

1 When customers' profit margins are hit hard, creating deep concern about costs, you can...
   - Provide a new service that helps them control costs.
   - Provide tools (checklists & templates) to reduce costs by optimizing overhead.
   - Help them choose the expense options that are justified by increased ROI in the timeframe that most fits their needs.

2 If your customers are making short-sighted decisions due to economic pressure, you can...

- Educate them on long-term strategies.
- Provide tools for weighing costs to benefits over near- and mid-term timelines.
- Improve the quality of the choices you provide, remaining sensitive to their needs.

3 When clients demand more, you have an invitation to...
- Step into a tighter relationship.
- Ask for more data to increase your ability to serve them.
- Customize your relationship to foster greater value to your clients.

You get the idea; you capitalize on their needs. Innovation experts recognize that market pressure always leads to progress; you just have to use the prevailing winds to sail forward!

These bold new competencies for leadership and strategy reveal a very different kind of game than association leaders have been playing, because frankly, the entire world of business is playing a new game. We're experiencing a new pace of disruption, a kind of leveling up. As change accelerates, innovations in leadership are emerging because they must. Rather than simply keep pace, tomorrow's leaders will often need to drive the changes they wish to see in the domains of organizational strategy and beyond.

And in terms of leadership, they'll need to *be* the change.

Association leaders stand before incredible opportunity fraught with rapidly shifting needs and radical technological disruption. In the pages ahead, we'll discuss both challenges and opportunities coming for associations, while simultaneously addressing some of society's greatest needs and the massive transformational opportunity on the horizon.

Working for the Benefit of Humanity

Select associations have begun to recognize the value of turning their mission toward the greater good of society. When they do, they expand their beneficiaries exponentially and open themselves to enormous value exchange with the larger world. This orientation tackles directly the pejorative common connotation of "special interests." While associations *are* special interests, they hold a concentration of collective knowledge, expertise, and power that can be brought to bear on larger social interests.

They're not alone in this shift. In early 2018, Laurence D. Fink, CEO of the world's biggest money manager, BlackRock[2], said this in his January statement:

> *"Society increasingly is turning to the private sector and asking that companies respond to broader societal challenges. Indeed, the public expectations of your company have never been greater. Society is demanding that companies, both public and private, serve a social purpose. To prosper over time, every company must not only deliver financial performance, but also show how it makes a positive contribution to society."*

As our world grows more complicated and changes in every sector multiply, it has become increasingly important that successful businesses contribute to humanity's greater good. Society has begun to demand it, and large-scale business success has begun to depend on it—in a way that was not true only ten years ago. Equally true: the state of our world now appears to depend on it.

These aims are reflected in the association model, too.

One of the greatest challenges for any organization is to accurately see threats on the horizon. After all, an existential threat can take you out; that's the very definition! If you're in the soda business, how do you embrace America's shifting mood toward health consciousness, namely growing demands for reduced sugar content?

The capacity to recognize an existential threat and respond to it proactively is exactly what Susan Neely harnessed in The Balance Calorie Initiative. CVS recognized their own disruptive threat as America began turning away from tobacco products. The retail giant's sales from those goods brought in $2 billiion a year, but by positioning themselves ahead of the trend they not only recouped more than they lost, they pulled ahead of their biggest competitor by demonstrating they cared enough to help America quit tobacco.

Still, all of this is easier said than done. So, how do you step free of denial and harness the headwinds to your benefit?

The Evolution of Associations

There are three evolutionary stages of associations: (1) transactional, (2) generative and (3) scalable.

The first stage I call *transactional*, because it's based on securing monetary advantage in the buying and selling of services for members of a discrete profession or trade. This was the beginning for associations, when a group of dedicated professionals pooled some of their resources to do more together than each could do alone. With their shared resources they could lobby, cull the best in education, stay abreast of developments in their field, monitor important statistics that helped them to grow and succeed,

Consider this strategy for cutting through the noise:

1 Pay attention to larger trends and identify those that challenge your market.

2 Reach out and ask those who matter most: run focus groups to get detailed information on emerging trends/existential threats, and dig into their underlying complexities.

3 Gather data. Pull together the facts on what is motivating consumers, how they view the issues, and potential partners who could work together with you on a broad solution to address the threat head-on.

4 Meet with neutral parties who are invested in the future everyone wants. Find an outside agency and convene a think-tank to identify potential solutions with an upside.

generate group buying discounts, garner discounted insurance, and so on.

The next stage is *generative*, because it literally generates new value. Here, associations move beyond simply providing discounts or group activity and begin bringing members together to forge new territory, i.e., create new value. This knowledge provides members with clear advantage of their peers and competitors and comes in two forms: deep knowledge and wide knowledge.

We deepen knowledge when we create new applications for existing experience and expertise. It takes what's already known and finds new ways to apply it, extending our abilities and absorbing new learning back into what we already know.

We widen knowledge when we broaden existing applications to adjacent fields, extending our domain laterally and opening up new areas to apply what we know.

The third evolutionary stage of associations is one I call *scalable*. Once here, an association scales the knowledge and experience of its members, allowing it to contribute to society as a whole. In addition to focusing our value on nurses, we provide the world with the experience and expertise of nurses. In addition to serving steel manufacturers, we provide the world with what it needs when it comes to the expertise and core value of steel manufacturers.

A scalable association parlays its niche into serving societal needs. It helps to make the world a better place by providing its insight and expertise—to better understand, integrate, and utilize its array of resources.

Visionary leaders recognize the evolutionary nature of these three stages, knowing that each successively builds beyond yet includes the qualities of the stages that came before. This means there are transactions at the core of generative organizations, and both transactions and generativity at the core of scalable associations.

There's power in this alignment. When you serve through transactions, generativity, *and* scalability, your stakeholders are aligned and new value streams are reinforced at each level, making them solid, robust, and dependable.

The innovation that leads to scalable associations requires risk, experimentation, and a new level of awareness by all players. It also requires uncovering new resources to fund and drive new activity at a whole new level of impact. That's why new leadership competencies are so important. In the next section, I'll identify some of these new competencies and provide guidance on how to develop them.

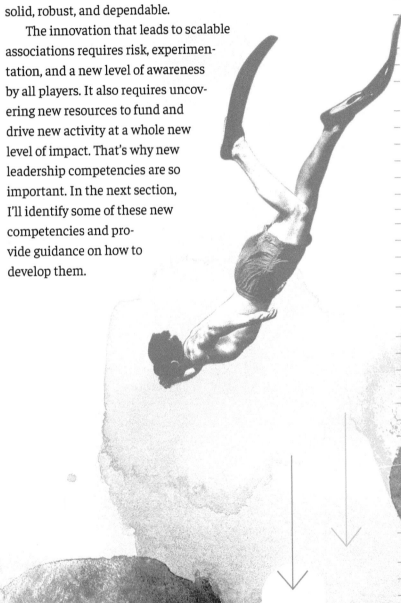

the road ahead promises ever more
disruption
and still greater
wonder

Two

VISIONARY LEADERSHIP COMPETENCIES

"A disruptive innovation is a technologically simple innovation in the form of a product, service, or business model that takes root in a tier of the market that is unattractive to the established leaders in an industry."

—Clayton Christensen, Harvard Business School

When the personal computer was first mass-marketed in the late 1970s, it wasn't immediately clear what it was good for beyond a tinkering toy for academics or an advanced typewriter for secretaries. But within a relatively short time it became clear that providing advanced computing power to the masses held enormous benefit—and would rapidly alter society. As I write this, fewer than 30 years have passed since the World Wide Web was made publicly available, yet its impact continues to dramatically disrupt industry after industry. Despite this rapid and radical technological change, we have all acclimated, often without noticing the effects or even stopping to consider what it might mean for the road ahead.

When we think of the future, we generally imagine a more brilliant version of today (or a more dystopian one, depending on our internal schemas). But exponential innovations are providing greater and greater potential to individuals and organizations, virtually reinventing what it means to be human. Hard as it may be to believe, we've barely begun, and the road ahead promises ever more disruption and still greater wonder. As the theoretical physicist Michio Kaku sagely wrote in the introduction to his bestseller, *Physics of the Future: How Science Will Shape Human Destiny and Our Lives by the Year 2100:* "The lesson here is that it is very dangerous to bet against the future."[3]

Virtually every sector is experiencing *exponential* change. Consider the accelerated growth of computing power due to rapid shrinking of the silicon chip; decreases in cost and size of digital devices; increase to human life expectancy over the last 100 years; increases in education expenditures in the U.S.; as well as the increase in people receiving high school and college education over the last 100 years, and more.[4] Our capabilities aren't simply improving; they're doubling, tripling, and quadrupling.

Coping with this accelerating speed of change requires different human skills from any we may have inherited from our ancestors or developed in the recent past. Over tens, or even hundreds of thousands of years, nearly everything humans encountered in their environment would have been virtually the same from one generation to the next. And yet for the first time in human history, children are growing up in a very new world—one with instant, unfettered access to unlimited data and information, as well as to virtually any other person in any other part of the world. Likewise, their parents—adults in their 30s and 40s today—have no experience with their parents' context. For example, they have never experienced rotary-dial phones or typewriters, nor did they go through America's civil rights movement or live in a age when most women remained at home. And what about their children? As change speeds up, our ability to adapt plays a major and largely unconscious role. Very soon, some humans may even be learning to live on Mars.

What Is the Exponential Future of Your Industry?

Wrapping Your Head Around Exponential Growth

Virtually every industry sector is experiencing exponential change. Coping with this accelerating pace of change requires leaders to develop skill at Imagining the Exponential. This exercise is designed to emphasize the need for shorter term and more intense thinking and planning.

Humans are famous for not being able to wrap our heads around exponential growth. We make the mistake of imagining the pace of the future to match the pace of the past. Yet, if the rate of progress doubles every ten years or so, we'll see changes in the next 90 years equivalent to the last 10,000 years, and in the next 100 years, changes equivalent to the last 20,000 years. Madness? After 7.5 years, the Human Genome Project had decoded only 1 percent of our genetic code. At that rate, another 743 years would be required to finish the job—but it was done in only 15 years.

Here's an exercise to help your team imagine what is possible when it comes to your sector. Using the form provided:

1. Make a list of achievements that took place within the last year in your field.

2. Think back to 10 years ago and note where the field was in those same areas.

3. Ask your leaders to extrapolate, based on that same pace of achievement, where your industry might be in 10 years.

4. Now ask them to imagine another 10 years for a total of 20 years in the future.

5. Repeat once more so that you're now imagining what miracles might happen in 30 years.

Timepoint	Achievements
10 years ago → STEP 2	
TODAY → STEP 1	
10 years IN THE FUTURE → STEP 3	
20 years IN THE FUTURE → STEP 4	
30 years IN THE FUTURE → STEP 5	

But remember that "exponential" means the speed of change doubles every year, so these five accounts are really:

- 10 years ago
- Today
- 5 years from now
- 5 + 2.5 = 7.5 years from now
- 5 + 2.5 + 1.25 = 8.75 years from now

So, change your table to read:

10 years ago
TODAY
~~*10*~~ **5** *years* IN THE FUTURE
~~*20*~~ **7.5** *years* IN THE FUTURE
~~*30*~~ **8.75** *years* IN THE FUTURE

Those outrageous 30-year predictions are likely to be here in fewer than 10 years!

Discuss the implications—not just for fun in imagining your future, but to probe: "What as yet uninvented technologies might we use to achieve our five-year goals?"

For much of the last century, technological and business changes have been exponential, but before those changes got to the sharp curve on the graph, we may have felt them as episodic or even as linear change. Consider the fax machine. It arrived in the late mid-century and completely up-ended communications technology, after which everything appeared to settle down for a time so we could all get back to business.

Then came desktops and laptops and email and cellphones and smartphones—and with them—constant, continuous change. (Say goodbye to the fax.) One new technology seems to arrive after the next, with hardly any time to catch our breath. Staff members are often wary and weary, repeating the common refrain: "When will this stop so we can get back to work?"

The speed of change will only continue to increase, so we must learn to conduct our strategy and execution in wholly new ways, requiring

new social, technological, and leadership competencies.

Of course, the answer is that it won't. This *is* the work.

Today's business leaders have to do more than steer their ships; they must adapt to a market that is morphing faster than any single person can digest or comprehend.

While leaders and entrepreneurs learn to adapt more quickly, they must do so while discerning what opportunities and advantages can be extracted from change in order to create new value propositions, without being diluted or overwhelmed in the process.

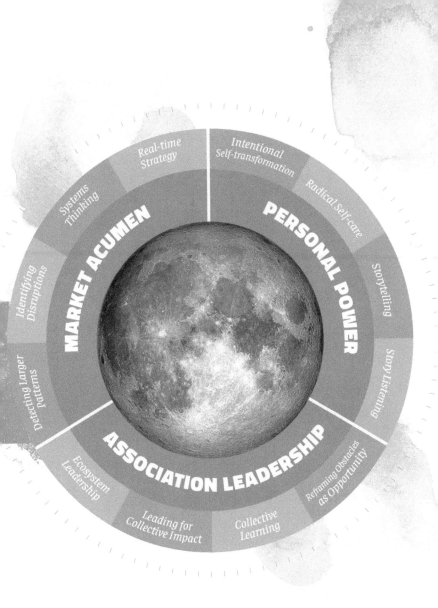

Twelve new visionary leadership competencies are required to do business in an exponential world. Coming up, I discuss each, paired with an application exercise. I have also placed them into three specific categories: Personal Power, Association

Leadership, and Market Acumen. Personal Power applies to those competencies that you as a leader must apply to yourself in order to lead with strength and force. Association Leadership refers to those competencies that are internal to your organization, enabling you to influence and develop your volunteers and staff. Market Acumen refers to those competencies that keep you in touch with the environment including emerging trends, customer expectations, and competition.

Personal Power

Intentional Self-transformation

Visionary leaders continuously seek to raise the caliber of their work by strengthening and expanding their competencies, capabilities, and range of influence. They recognize that their real-world results are directly rooted in their personal mental models, and that by transforming their performance they can positively and often powerfully impact their organizations. Truly great leaders make this an art form, diving into new experiences that catalyze deep and intentional personal growth and change for themselves and their most valuable partners, including their board of directors and senior leadership team.

Three Steps to Increase Your Capability as a Leader

1 Identify the skills or mindsets you wish you had;

2 Find leaders today who exhibit those traits;

3 Spend face-to-face time with them. Fly to their city, take them out for a meal, discuss their passion.

Radical Self-care

With increased stress, the priority of peak performance is elevated. Every true leader is called upon through multiple channels of communication and around the clock. To operate effectively, all methods of support are required. Each of us is a node in a much larger web; we cannot operate with integrity or maximum impact unless we're in the best possible condition—physically, psychologically, emotionally, and spiritually. Those leaders who are able to bring the full force of their insight and action to bear on complex challenges are those who sustain their performance through regular and deeply effective self-care. They're aligned to the priorities that feed and sustain them and make it a conscious priority to see they stay in peak condition on all levels.

Workaholism is unsustainable; it taxes the system, causing severe imbalances. When dedication and long hours are complimented by soul-sustaining renewal, it's possible to *hurry up and slow down so you can go faster.*[5]

How to Impact Performance with Radical Self-care

Identify area(s) where radical self-care would make the biggest impact on your ability to perform:

Physically —Are you tired or regularly in pain?

Psychologically —Are there certain issues you find you're unable to take on productively?

Emotionally —Do you often feel irritable, angry, moody, or unhappy?

Spiritually —Do you find yourself drained before end-of-day, or feeling as though no matter what you do, you just can't get ahead? Do your efforts feel disconnected from a larger sense of purpose?

Stories are powerful for two very important reasons:
1 they are memorable and easily repeated, and
2 they form the smallest portable context; i.e., they convey the minimum amount of information necessary to transpose learning from one situation to another.

  While working at the World Bank I helped to lead a series of think tanks that brought together our staff with those of Disney, HP, Ernst & Young, Accenture, the International Storytelling Center and Eastman Chemical. Steven Denning, my boss at the time, coined the term "springboard story" to identify the kind of stories that spark action. Springboard stories communicate a specific call to action by describing an incident where that

Learn to Tell Stories that Travel

Every leader wants their case for change to be easy to understand and memorable. Unfortunately, most rely on PowerPoint or worse, spreadsheets. These tools work well when coupled with a good story but can even cause damage when traveling without one.

  The best thing you can do to hone your own storytelling chops is to listen for short, memorable stories that come your way. Notice which ones stick in your own mind after a day or two and practice telling them to others.

  Here's an example I use to drive home how memorable stories are:

  I like to camp. One year I took my dog into the Adirondack wilderness. When we arrived, I noticed he was weaving and foaming at the mouth. Immediately I recalled a story I heard on NPR **three**

action has already taken place. The story features a protagonist your listeners can easily identify with. The story includes enough details to be authentic and memorable, but is stripped of unnecessary detail. It concludes with a happy ending and an invitation to listeners to imagine the results that could be achieved if they respond to the call to action.[6]

In those think tanks, we looked at the use of storytelling in modern organizations and found powerful applications that included sparking behavior change, building trust, sharing knowledge, and more. Every leader would do well to learn how to tell stories that are short, impactful and easy to share.

I include Storytelling, along with Story Listening, under the category of Personal Power because these competencies increase your ability to influence others.

years earlier that told me he could have flipped his stomach. If I was right, he needed surgery within a few hours to survive.

See how my brain recalled relevant information when it was needed, using a story I heard on the radio years before?

But wait... if I moved on to my next topic, what would you most want to know? *What happened to the dog?!* See how you are hooked by the story. That's what you want your listeners to be... waiting with baited breath for the conclusion of your story. As long as they are waiting, you have their attention. So, here's the happy ending:

Thanks to an open veterinary clinic in the area my dog was operated on and lived many more years to enjoy numerous other camping trips.

All good storytellers start as curious story listeners. It is important that you not only practice identifying stories that other leaders use, but that you ask your stakeholders about their own experience.

This is a source of personal power because it is a method for gaining insight into the people you care about. With the wisdom you glean from their anecdotes you can build trust, forge new relationships, and develop new ways of serving them.

Good listeners are hard to come by. Picking up this skill is one of the best ways to develop your ability to lead *from behind*.

Listening to Understand

The best way to dig deep into another's story is to start by asking them to tell it. "I would like to know more about why it's important to you to come to our meetings. Can you tell me about a specific time something happened in a meeting that made you wanted to talk about it with others?"

Then, lean in and listen beneath the words. We know that the text someone shares offers only a fraction of the content. It's the way they speak, which words they emphasize, how they string their sentences together. Their body language amplifies that content. Use your eyes, ears, and heart to see if you can discern what it is they care most about. Then respond along these lines:

I am really interested in what you learned in that situation. Can you unpack that for me?

That sounded really important. Please tell me more about that.

That's not immediately obvious for me; can you fill in the blanks? Why was that important?

In Nelson Mandela's great autobiography, *Long Walk to Freedom*, he admires an axiom, "...a leader... is like a shepherd. He stays behind the flock, letting the most nimble go out ahead, whereupon the others follow, not realizing that all along they are being directed from behind."

When a key constituent recounts an important story, dig into it. Ask questions to learn more. Put yourself in their shoes. See the world through their eyes. This is a critical skill that leads to increased personal power because it allows you to sense what is most important to the people you count on. Once you know what they value, you are in a position to create the conditions for them to achieve it, and by doing so, deepen your relationship.

Association Leadership

Reframing Obstacles as Opportunity

It is all too common for idealism to be stifled by the fear associated with risk. Yet, educated risk is the very nature of seizing opportunity. Peter Diamandis, multi-entrepreneur and founder of XPRIZE, says, "The world's biggest problems are the world's biggest business opportunities."[7] As associations consider committing to scalability, they must necessarily convert intractable problems into great opportunities—changing as if by alchemy the challenges they take on to reveal the massive potential inside.

To do this successfully, association leaders must learn the visionary art of reframing, engaging in dialog that opens peoples' minds. Reframing isn't preaching. Rather, it involves unbelievers in meaningful interaction that leads to a reexamination of assumptions. It births new contexts in which the original obstacles plus a new mindset can shape the way toward deep opportunity. Reframing is proactive and mutual. It includes outreach activities such as convening groups of stakeholders and designing liberating structures to deal with the most difficult issues, converting them into a set of circumstances that make comprehensive and wide-sweeping solutions possible.

Obstacle Judo

Judo practitioners are taught to take on an attack by swiftly and skillfully rerouting their opponent's energy so that both they and their attacker are repositioned without harm. This makes Judo a beautiful metaphor for finding opportunity in obstacles.

Every upset is a new circumstance that, viewed opportunistically, has the potential to serve your aims. Consider some examples:

Obstacle: Shaken by a contracting market, your customers put the brakes on their purchases.

Response: Provide assistance on long-term strategies, including help with planning, cost-benefit analysis, financing, and ways to invest in your services for best possible short-term gains.

Exercise:

1 List your most pressing obstacles;

2 Distribute to your senior team and ask each to submit three unique ways to leverage these obstacles as opportunities;

3 Bring the team together to go through their responses, using the power of collective thinking to develop the most promising ideas for action.

Collective Learning

When seeking solutions to systemic problems, outcomes will be unpredictable and ever-changing. Results will never be prescriptive technical fixes that can be known in advance, although in certain cases they may be intuited. Instead, as the future unfolds, the pace of change will continue to reveal more challenges, more complexities, and more opportunity, and solution models will emerge only as understanding deepens. Often, even the most expert strategy will be upended by sudden disruptions no one could have predicted.

Visionary leaders create learning organizations. They foster and facilitate an environment of mutual trust and a rich investment in mission. Where this occurs, real-time collective learning emerges. For visionary organizations, a spirit of collective aspiration over and above individual competition pushes through. It generates trust and engagement, holding the organization in an evolutionary dynamic of strength so that complexity and change aren't felt as destabilizing forces of entropy, but as energizing powers for co-creation. There is a leaning-in together, an energy of excitement where senior leaders are enlivened by the challenges and by one another.

Four Steps to Increase Impact through Collaboration

1 Identify an issue that would benefit from collaboration;

2 Behind the scenes (without mentioning "collaboration"), bring your leaders together and ask them how their combined roles could advance the issue;

3 Identify at least four paths forward which involve working together;

4 Ask your leaders to follow up and bring you their results.

New forms of organizational partnerships are emerging as the world becomes more and more interconnected and the problems humanity takes on are greater in scope and direr in consequence. Collective impact[8] is a new kind of collaboration that relies on multiple and varied organizations partnering with activists and the public to create results. Collective impact relies first and foremost on establishing a common agenda, a clear vision of a future state that every contributor is passionately invested in. This includes a future that commercial organizations rely on, as well as a world that activists deeply care about. Articulating and defending the common agenda is the organizing force behind collective impact, along with the ability to achieve transparent communication and clear, common metrics. Most important is the ability to work in a democratic environment where partners pool their resources, expertise, and experience.

More details on the collective impact method appear in Chapter 4.

We have gone from connected to hyper-connected and from interconnected to interdependent.

—Thomas Friedman

John Kania and Mark Kramer first wrote about collective impact in the *Stanford Social Innovation Review* (2011), identifying five key elements:

1 *Common agenda* – a shared understanding of the problem along with an agreed-upon approach to solving it by working together.

2 *Mutually reinforcing actions* that participants execute to realize the common agenda.

3 *Metrics* that are the same across all parties involved.

4 *Communication* so everyone knows what's going on and what progress is being made.

5 *Backbone organization* – serves the entire initiative and coordinates activity.

The *Stanford Social Innovation Review* houses major articles and thought leadership on collective impact.

VISIT SSIR.ORG AND SEARCH "COLLECTIVE IMPACT" FOR A TREASURE TROVE OF KNOWLEDGE.

Ecosystem Leadership

Leaders today work with multiple overlapping constituencies simultaneously—the board of directors; executive committee; other committees; influential volunteers; industry and professional thought leaders; the media; the public; partner organizations; suppliers; and others. Social networks are notoriously unwieldy.

Further complicating the situation is that associations lack the insularity that private sector organizations enjoy, so that communication crosses boundaries much more easily. These are open ecosystems of influencers, and the complexity of relationships, the history of concerns, and the politics of action can all combine to seem overwhelming.

How many times have you heard volunteer leaders or senior staff say, "I don't do politics"? What they're really saying is: "I'm sticking my head in the sand because that's the only way I know how to get my job done."

This must change.

The skills inherent in balancing shifting priorities over groups of invested parties must move to the foreground for association leaders to generate the results our world needs. It is the job of leaders to convene multiple groups of stakeholders around critical issues that deliver solid value to the members and beneficiaries of all parties. This takes special skills many of today's leaders lack, including the ability to craft a common agenda, à la collective impact, so that it's compelling from multiple perspectives, including, most importantly, the members and the public good.

Ecosystem Leadership for Collective Impact

Task your leaders with crafting a *common agenda* for multiple groups inside your organization. Ask them to use this common agenda to convene several constituencies to work together on one of your most important projects. Provide the team with information on collective impact, and ask them to run the initiative as a way to build their capacity for collective impact initiatives that include partners outside your organization.

A key document to share is *"Collective Impact,"* (found here: *https://ssir.org/articles/entry/collective_impact).*

Market Acumen

Detecting Larger Patterns

As new change combinations manifest in the marketplace, distinct and overarching patterns will arise, some with gargantuan proportions—artificial intelligence; communication and connectivity; social technologies; autonomous transportation; cybersecurity; and more. Visionary business leaders strive to discern those world changes that present lasting and comprehensive impact—the *mega*-trends. They sharpen a skillset for sensing rate of decay and determining interdependent consequences. The people who become adept at determining which changes can be built upon versus those that will dissolve too quickly will be the people able to generate new applications with a half-life long enough to justify investment.

How to Identify Megatrends

Five questions to help your senior leaders identify megatrends:

1 What disruptions have been game changers in our field over the last one, two, and three years?

2 What new development might change the way we make money forever?

3 What emerging trends might work together to make our sector a small subset of another sector?

4 What is threatening to permanently disrupt ou customers'/ members' lives today?

5 If we were going to start a business today to take all our customers away forever, what business would we start?

It's important to note that this goes beyond identifying specific trends as they gain currency. Detecting larger patterns is about larger, overarching movements that combine innovations into a global game change. For example, with the rise of personal and pocket computers and the Internet, we have entered the era of ubiquitous, instant communication, where everyone can share knowledge and information with everyone else 24/7 in a frictionless environment.

Identifying Disruptions

It is critical to distinguish disruptive from sustaining innovations. Sustaining innovations are all about improving upon existing value, making your products and services better. Disruptive innovations are game-changers. They mostly start out small in the contained markets of early adopters. But disruptive innovations iterate fast and can quickly gain speed, overtaking stalwarts and industry giants, causing even the "too big to fail" to collapse. A critical leadership competency is understanding disruptions—where they start and how to identify those that threaten to topple your value propositions.

Three recommendations for spotting future disruptions today:

1 *Disruptions start small.*
   Identify the smallest start-ups competing in your space.

2 *Disruptions run lean and mean.*
   What new services or products have you passed by because you're unable to make a decent profit from them?

3 *Disruptions pick up traction as they grow.*
   What's growing its way into your space? And how is it fundamentally different? (The iPod was not just a better Walkman. It enabled the creation of iTunes, which changed the music industry forever and became a primary revenue stream for Apple.)

Systems Thinking

Even in democratic cultures, we're accustomed to dualistic two-party fragmentation, where sharp polarization exists and black-and-white thinking reigns supreme. Everyone takes a side, and each side is adamant its own view is correct. Even where consensus-building efforts emerge, they can be time-consuming and prone to failure. As the pace of change accelerates, dualistic thinking and left/right power struggles simply can't hold up to the mounting complexities we face.

The shortcomings of political thinking—either liberal or conservative, either Republican or Democrat—is not the only example of restrictive and incomplete binary thinking. Every binary (either/or) construct is fatally restricted. Systems thinking starts with a series of AND statements, identifying opposing trends as part of the same set and sidestepping judgment or option-eliminating decisions. The resulting list gives a holistic or multidimensional perspective that more accurately describes our complex world.

Systems thinking is the evolving 21st century capacity to see, understand, and communicate about multidimensional and multidisciplinary models and the phenomena they generate. As a result of data intelligence and advanced research methods, the world we are able to perceive has opened up. Medical researchers are learning to see the influential matrix created by age, nationality, race, and socioeconomic health. They add to that matrix complex genetic factors, detailed histories, environmental conditions, and even personal experiences of childhood trauma. They work with the intricate causal fabric these factors and others play in the creation of disease.

For example, environmental researchers are baffled to discover the mind-blowing degree to which plant and animal biodiversity are positively impacted after wolves[9] have been reintroduced to a habitat, and even the startling impact their reintroduction can have on the path of rivers. Each of these systems overlaps, creating a more complex and accurate picture of the health or disease of still other systems.

Learning to foster systems awareness allows leaders and their organizations greater agency and sharper predictive and reflexive reasoning. Wherever systemic forces emerge, a problem will have many variables—multiple causes, multiple symptoms, and changing outcomes—which black-and-white, single-solution frameworks fail miserably to describe or to solve.

The complex problems we face today require us to propose sets of potential solutions in new and original ways, and those we face tomorrow necessitate a deeper way of seeing our world and of listening to one another.

How to Practice Systems Thinking

1 Pick an issue you feel strongly about and write out your position in one short paragraph;

2 Now, take the polar opposite view. You don't have to agree; that's not the point. Do your best to write out the polar opposite view as if it were an authentic attempt at explaining the dilemma, in one short paragraph;

3 Next, pick a hybrid view that combines *both* positions. Write it out in one short paragraph, again, as if it were an authentic attempt to understand and explain;

4 Examine all three views to see how they reinforce each other and how each creates circumstances which bolster the other perspectives. List these reinforcements in short descriptions of no more than two sentences each;

5 Draw a picture that illustrates the three views and their reinforcements. Don't skip this step! It's important to use another part of your brain to look at the system;

6 Review your original position to see if any aspect has changed as a result of the process;

7 Finally, given your overview, list the actions that you can take to advance the issue in the direction you'd like to see it go.

Caveat for this exercise: be careful not to push ambiguity away through a desire to simplify or see your way materialize. Ambiguity, uncomfortable as it often is, represents a condition of the environment that should not be brushed away, but tolerated and explored for its value.

Embedded in associations today is the periodic review of strategy—the organizational effort to collect intelligence and bring together the board in order to reexamine the marketplace and adapt operations in light of the mission and current circumstances. But like everything else, these periodic assessments are disrupted by accelerating change. Associations are called to move faster than their scheduled strategic planning can address.

Able leaders know this intuitively. Some of the most innovative association CEOs I work with make up for this gap in strategic evaluation through regular communication with board members, thought leaders, influential volunteers, and senior staff. They generate multi-player feedback circuits which give rise to complex adaptive behavior for the organization.

Overall, obligatory and periodic strategic planning meetings create a tax on leadership, while perpetuating the pretense that all bases are covered. In response, new business models must emerge which allow continuous streams of intelligence to inform overarching plans, and where dynamic flexibility is integrated into the organization, providing nimble and entrepreneurial responses to inflection points that matter.

Visionary leaders are masters at listening to their organizations, monitoring for intelligent systems feedback, and leaning into the future to hear what is coming. They don't do this alone; they share leadership with valued peers and are wise enough to look everywhere inside their organizations for new leadership instincts—not just from the "usual suspects."

Real-time strategy is connected to intentional self-transformation, collective learning, and systems thinking. Indeed, all visionary leadership competencies are interconnected. Chapter 3 delves deeper into real-time strategy in the age of disruption.

Real-time Strategy Practicum

To build the capacity for real-time strategy, try this:

1 Introduce a segment at your weekly senior leadership team meetings called "Opportunity Identification," with the description: *Identify and share opportunities that would accelerate achievement of our strategic goals. To qualify, an opportunity must shorten the time to achievement by 30 days or more.*

2 Ask participants to share their ideas in five minutes or less, rewarding those who introduce legitimate opportunities with immediate praise.

3 When a great opportunity is identified, fold it immediately into the work program.

4 Over the course of six months, tally the total time saved and share it with the team. If successful, you will be able to continuously shorten time-to-achievement.

The twelve competencies discussed here prepare leaders and the groups they lead for more effective collaboration with and influence on the systems in which they must operate. In my work with executive leadership teams (both boards of directors and C-level teams), I have discovered the importance of doing the above exercises as a team. It is critical to build these competencies at the team level for leadership modeling and developing the shared mindset that can lead to better ideation and more effective execution.

In addition, I have developed an assessment from diagnostic comparisons across my clients and body of work. It can be found along with the evaluation notes in the Appendix, and on my website at **VisionaryLeadership.com/thebook.** You have my permission to copy/download this assessment and distribute it. I encourage you to take the assessment and create an executive action plan to develop your visionary leadership skills.

I have also found this assessment to provide excellent guidance for the Board of Directors and the executive team. I suggest you use this as an at your next retreat, handing out the assessment and the evaluation. After everyone has completed it, you may go through the competencies to discuss your team's areas of strength and weakness.

You may also send me your board's or your executive team's assessment and I will provide an interpretation of their results. Email them to Seth@VisionaryLeadership.com

For your convenience, the evaluation is also presented here. The rating tool appears at the front of this book. How did you do? Copy your scores here, then consider my recommendations.

Real-time
Strategy

Intentional
Self-transformation

Systems
Thinking

Radical Self-care

MARKET ACUMEN

PERSONAL POWER

Identifying
Disruptions

Storytelling

Detecting Larger
Patterns

Stop Listening

Ecosystem
Leadership

ASSOCIATION LEADERSHIP

Reframing Obstacles
as Opportunity

Leading for
Collective Impact

Collective
Learning

Assessment Evaluation

Personal Power ⟶ (___ TOTAL SCORE)

16 or below: Your development is limiting your performance and your organization's potential. It is time to make your personal power a priority. Raise your game by getting involved in activities that stretch your self-development well beyond your comfort zone.

17 to 31: You have some skill when it comes to personal power but will still benefit by getting out of your comfort zone. Make some new friends who are creating results well beyond your own and enroll in an adventure that stretches your limits.

32 and above: You a high-performing leader. By taking your development seriously, you are investing in your ability to create extraordinary results. You have the leadership firepower it takes to be a visionary and follow it up with action.

Association Leadership ⟶ (___ TOTAL SCORE)

16 or below: Your leadership style is stale and generates equally stale organizational outcomes. Invest in yourself. Take a leadership course in which over half the participants are better leaders than you. Seek out peers who are doing better than you at creating exceptional results and learn from them.

17 to 31: You have solid skills but are still short on the visionary scale. It's time for you to take on a project that is so ambitious it intimidates you. Surround yourself with partners, colleagues, and leaders who have consistently generated bigger, bolder results than you have. Step up. Build your capacity to lead.

32 and above: You are a visionary leader for your association. You have positioned yourself and your organization to lead with exceptional results. Mentor others.

Market Acumen ⟶ ⟨ ____ TOTAL SCORE ⟩

16 or below: You are out of touch with today's market and your organization is vulnerable as a result. Dedicate time to studying the market: including members, potential members, partners, and competitors. Identify the trends most likely to upset your association's value proposition. Study how to increase the impact of your mission using new tools and techniques that have been developed in the last two years. Push yourself harder to understanding the market and how it influences your success.

17 to 31: You have some skill at understanding the market environment, but you could do better. Raise the bar. Dig deeper into the news. Identify thought leaders and reach out to them personally. Involve yourself in conversations with movers and shakers. Listen more than you speak. Ask close friends how you can up your game.

32 and above: You are a market maven. Share your knowledge and expertise with colleagues. Increase the leaders you are mentoring. Develop your ability to execute. Perfect your market moves.

speed

time

disruption

innovation

scale

partnership

Three

REAL-TIME STRATEGY IN THE AGE OF DISRUPTION

"Most long-range forecasts of what is technically feasible in future time periods dramatically underestimate the power of future developments because they are based on what I call the 'intuitive linear' view of history rather than the 'historical exponential' view."
—Ray Kurzweil, Director of Engineering, Google

Every leader I know works at full steam.

There's more to do than can be done, so it's execution, execution, execution. With everything moving so fast, new options emerge in the market with unprecedented speed. A key question for a busy leader, then, is how to identify priorities in real time, so your team can seize opportunity and drive results where it matters most?

If you fail to rise with them, your members and partners will go elsewhere—and these days, that can be as easy as a click.

The topple rate is the rate at which the group of companies leading a given market or industry loses the leadership position. According to Deloitte,[10] the topple rate steadily increased in the US from 1965 to 2009. And although it dropped in 2011, it's on the rise again. Everyone hunts for value and customers shift like schools of fish wherever innovations emerge to satisfy unmet needs. Pervasive multi-billion-dollar enterprises like Amazon set the bar. Smartphones and tablets make it easy to find what you need when you need it, no matter the provider. Thought leadership has become a commodity, no longer driving sales. Even if you're the best in your business, a Google search displays you as just another resource. Potential members may consume your intellectual property without moving any closer to buying.

For some, these forces spell the beginning of the end. Through complacency or sheer overwhelm, they plod along at a predetermined periodicity with strategic planning exercises, pretending they can catch up or even advance by taking long breaks between thinking about their position in the market and how to get ahead.

But for others, the very same forces drive an unrelenting pursuit of leadership. Successful leaders are those who learn to do strategy in real time.

From my work with 100-plus CEOs (and many boards and senior management teams) across the association spectrum, I've observed that the most successful do the following:

- *Become hypervigilant for disruption.* They build talent and business processes that can spot new growth and developing threats through strategic foresight, and introduce, then iterate their own disruptive micro-initiatives incubated in mini-economies.

- *Turn their value outward through scalable impact.* In so doing, they harness the unique value of their members' experience and expertise, leveraging it for massive audiences.

- *Build the fleet of stakeholders that drive change.* These stakeholders create the connective tissue and a common agenda among their board of directors, key partners, member influencers, senior leadership team, and activists.

· *Get serious about the digital business imperative.* By doing so, successful leaders overcome foundational issues once and for all, accelerate innovation with new data points, deliver value through new channels, and anticipate the emerging trends that will impact their members' work and lives.

And they do it all concurrently and continuously.

Visionary leaders don't simply take a snapshot every third year or pretend the market will be stable for the next five. They may hold periodic board sessions dedicated to this work, but the best of the best practice real-time strategy. In Part I, I profiled an executive on his success with shifting from periodic strategic planning to real-time strategy. His work stands as an example of the behaviors described above.

Those associations that succeed in a rapidly changing disruptive market will train their leaders to move strategy to real time. When the future hits your door every hour, sometimes every minute, flexible continual strategy is the only way to stay ahead of the curve.

Let's take a look at *five practices that lead to real-time strategy* and their requirements. The resulting big picture will provide insight into how leading-edge associations practice it.

The five practices are:
1. DEALING WITH DISRUPTION;
2. INSTITUTING STRATEGIC FORESIGHT;
3. DRIVING DIGITAL BUSINESS;
4. SCALING FOR IMPACT;
5. CREATING NEW TYPES OF PARTNERSHIPS.

The first three practices are the subject of this chapter, where we focus on what it takes to achieve real-time strategy in the age of disruption. This work prepares an association to take on Grand Challenges, the subject of Chapter 4. This is where the last two practices are discussed.

Practice 1. Dealing with Disruption

Disruption has become a regular feature of the marketplace, for better or worse. Silicon Valley entrepreneurs have an interest in frictionless renewable revenue—another name for subscription business models. As a result, they have associations in their sights. Anytime an organization can capture an entire demographic by meeting unmet needs, disruption occurs. Entrepreneurs don't wait until the light of day to strike, and astute association leaders never rest on their laurels when it comes to spotting potential disruptions or introducing their own. However, there's one big obstacle most associations face.

While associations have mastered execution, they've fumbled disruptive innovation. *The same reason associations are so good at repeatable processes and incremental improvement causes them to be challenged by game-changing value creation.*

The mindset of efficiently executing a repeatable task for a large base of customers is the very frame-of-thinking that intentionally looks away from small market incursions with lean margins which may provide new ways of serving up value. Said another way, your expertise in meetings, education, buyers' clubs, publications, and every other service you provide regularly, is likely screening out the very game-changing models that excite your members and compel them to try something altogether different. This is why the leadership competencies mentioned in the previous chapter are so important and need to be encouraged in your senior management team and board of directors.

Disruptions in your market start small and grow quickly. Early detection and monitoring is imperative. School your leaders, volunteers, and staff in the importance of finding business incursions before they grow into a threat. I developed this Threat Assessment Protocol for organizations swimming through turbulent seas. It relies on two stages of threat assessment. Stage 1 is used to determine if the threat requires a significant response. If so, Stage 2 is called for.

Stage 1 Threat Assessment Protocol:

1 *Threat Identification*

An incursion-in-the-making is identified. An incursion-in-the-making is anything serving unmet customer needs in your space. It could be new technology available for exploitation, a change in demographics among your customers, a demographic you serve emerging as a target audience for a competitor, or anything else, large or small, that shifts the playing field away from you.

2 *Threat Assessment Meeting*

The senior management team assembles, or an agenda item is added to an upcoming session. The point is raised in advance and people are put on alert that a Threat Assessment will take place so they can prepare accordingly.

3 *Explore Challenges/Opportunities*

Each participant prepares for the meeting by completing three statements:
a "This change in circumstance raises these important issues for our customers and our organization ..."
b "The areas most likely to be impacted are..."
c "Possible challenges/opportunities include..."

Each of these challenges and opportunities may generate enough value in the market to justify your investment in a significant innovation. At this early stage of the Threat Assessment, options don't need to be realistic or even seem achievable. It's too early in the process to pass judgment; there's not enough information. All possibilities should be identified and explored.

4 *Value Assessment*

The agenda goes through four steps:

a The person who identified the change in circumstance speaks up to share the change they identified and why they feel it warrants a Threat Assessment.

b Each of the other members shares their own three statements.

c Open discussion ensues to identify what can be done near-term to monitor the situation, including identification of key indicators to determine what may be maturing into a legitimate threat.

d A decision is called for: Does this deserve further consideration? Do these circumstances warrant our continued monitoring and possible action?

- If no, it's done. The Threat Assessment is over.
- If yes, a Stage 2 Threat Assessment meeting is scheduled and individuals are designated to take accountability for further developing those ideas that warrant serious consideration.

Stage 2 Threat Assessment:

The Stage 2 Threat Assessment only takes place when the first meeting clearly identified opportunities worthy of the group's time and consideration. These sessions can happen in the same day if an identified threat is imminent.

The purpose of this follow-up is to deepen knowledge among the team and determine if significant action is required. This is particularly helpful when a disruption has occurred which could be used to maximum advantage or represents an extreme incursion into your business.

The Stage 2 Threat Assessment agenda goes through 5 steps:

1 *Meeting convenes.*

Participants arrive ready to negotiate resource allocation. This means they bring their budgets and calendars and are ready to lobby, defend, and commit resources.

2 *Context and purpose are stated.*

The meeting leader recaps the initial Threat Assessment meeting including:
a The initial idea;
b Highlights of the discussion;
c Why it was determined that a Stage 2 Threat Assessment is required;
d Who was designated to take accountability for further developing the ideas warranting serious consideration.

3 *Presentations are made.*

Each person designated to further develop ideas makes a presentation of no more than 10-15 minutes. Presentations include both narrative and supporting data. The narrative tells the story of what they investigated; why it was chosen; what they hoped to learn; what they were able to gather; and the conclusions they have drawn. Supporting data is shared.

All presentations are made prior to opening the floor to discussion. Presentations are short and to the point with additional time for clarifying questions.

4 *Open discussion and option identification.*

The group discusses and debates with the express purpose of identifying the threat to be addressed. At the conclusion of the discussion, options are identified.

5 *Decisions are made for each option: pursue or not.*

The decision process depends upon the organization and the option under discussion. Final decisions are generally made in one of three ways: by the leader, by the leader with input from the team, or by a majority vote.

With a decision, the following questions are answered:
a What is the objective?
b What are the next steps?
c Who is responsible for each?
d What resources are required for success?
e How will progress be evaluated?

These two processes, Threat Assessment and Stage 2 Threat Assessment, provide a format that can be used when a threat intrudes where there is little time to react. Often there's anxiety in the air, making it hard to think clearly. Before redirecting costly resources or making decisions that result in a significant strategic shift, these processes provide ad hoc due diligence to ensure you're not going off on a wild jag, but in fact have located a genuine impending threat.

If disruption is going to remain a regular feature of the environment—and there is no question that it will—then to maintain their lead, associations must develop their own disruptions. How? By building the internal capacity to introduce prototypes into micro-markets and rapidly develop the successes that expand their reach and value. This requires new competencies for senior managers who regularly extend their reach beyond the known, fishing for the compelling value propositions that will grow their market.

In fact, disruptive innovations generally arise in clusters since many are made possible by combining existing offerings and capitalizing on new capabilities that reach a threshold of affordability in the marketplace. When the technology for self-driving cars matured, self-driving trucks and mass transit weren't far behind. Mashing new technologies together with unmet consumer needs creates overlapping opportunities, which means new products and services come in waves. Periodic evaluation of the market completely misses these waves of new value generation unless serendipitously and perfectly timed—not a gamble you want to take.

Dealing with disruption has no periodicity; innovation doesn't emerge in a cycle

Associations that learn to identify small breakthroughs and rapidly iterate will be best prepared for new forms of member value creation. This capability is built through rigorous forms of *strategic foresight*—business processes that continuously identify emerging trends, secondary impacts, and ripening discomfort among key constituencies.

A disruptive prototype is a product or service that changes the game with just enough features to satisfy early customers while providing the proper feedback for future product or service development. To succeed, your prototype must sell. Otherwise, it isn't viable.

Here's one way to create a disruptive prototype:

1 Develop a set of product or service ideas based on talking to your strategists, doing environment scans, and analyzing the results;

2 Share these ideas with customers to see where the most enthusiasm occurs. Be ready to make changes based on their responses. You're going for maximum uptake, so pay close attention to their input;

3 Get as clear as possible about what features you are providing to your customers with your prototype. Identify the features that cause them to react with, "I've got to have this!";

4 Sort the features on your list into two categories. First, identify those features you must get right in order for your product to sell. Second, identify what innovations you're testing. In other words, what features are you betting your prototype on? These two categories can overlap;

5 Put together the minimum amount of features that will give your early adopters satisfaction. You must ensure these features deliver results from the start. However, this isn't the time to polish things up or add bells and whistles. You are creating what's called a *minimum viable product* with your prototype.

Now it's time to conduct a small, controlled roll-out:

1 Put the offering together and do several (a minimum of three) trial runs as if you were the customer. Learn and upgrade these until you consistently get the customer experience right.

2 Begin providing your prototype to a set of customers. Track customer interaction through marketing, sales, and any support you're called on to provide to your customers when they make use of your prototype.

   In particular, watch for:
   a How fast customers grasp what you're offering;
   b Whether they use it for what you intended, or something else;
   c How fast they put it to use;
   d Their success with the new offering;
   e How enthusiastic they are about continuing to use it.

3 Now you're left with two different potential scenarios:

   Scenario 1: If your prototype fails, find out why. Study your customers' behavior and interview them to see what went wrong, then determine if it's salvageable. Don't be afraid to fail. Failing fast speeds up your learning—and your eventual success.

   Scenario 2: If your prototype succeeds, find out what can be improved. Get to work on the next iteration!

It should be noted that for a prototype to succeed initially, it doesn't have to generate enough revenue to justify itself in your regular offerings. In the early stages, it's more important that you successfully address unmet customer needs. Through iteration you will grow the profitable revenue.

Practice 2

Instituting Strategic Foresight

Through the practice of strategic foresight, we peer into the future, taking in the rising and falling of emerging trends and correlating them to our customers' needs. Strategic foresight done well and continuously allows you to see new potential solutions as they emerge on the horizon.

We all know we have to keep our eyes on what's next, whether the news comes to us from the Internet, a cocktail conversation, a thought leader's analysis, traditional news sources, social media, or in flashes of insight as we integrate key new information. But we can make this process more efficient.

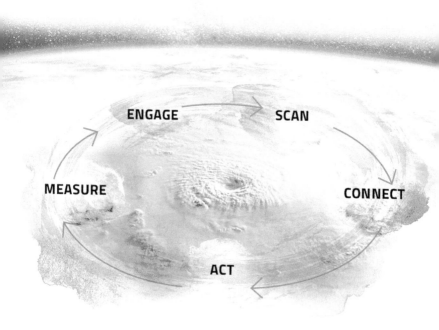

ENGAGE → SCAN

MEASURE

CONNECT

ACT

Organizations hell-bent on seizing the future and holding on engage in continuous strategic foresight. They task staff and key members with execution and work with their strategists continuously.

How to Engage Strategic Foresight

Consider the following process:

1 *Deploy your strategists.*
   Reach out and invite players in-the-know into the process, including your senior team, strategy-minded staff members, your board of directors, strategic thinking members, and thought leaders. Involve them in your organization's success, especially when it comes to studying the future, identifying unmet needs, identifying what others are doing to create breakthroughs, and designing your own prototypes of disruptive innovation.

2 *Scan the environment.*
   Collect emerging trends and information in three different areas:
   a *Your business model* – Find out what's shaking when it comes to how organizations are ringing the cash register among trade associations or professional societies.
   b *Your industry* – Discover the latest breakthroughs in your sector, profession, or industry.
   c *Your customers' lives* – Remember the executive mentioned on pages 25 who hired for managers who could do strategy in real time? When the market was thrown into turmoil, the executive went to help his customers. He found out what they needed and discerned how to provide it. Every business owner must stay in touch with their customers' needs.

3 *Connect the dots.*
   Share the results of your environmental scans with your strat-

egists and get their reactions. You can do this by bringing them all together, or you can run things past them singly. Remember, you don't want to sacrifice the quality of your intelligence for logistical ease or the periodicity of meetings. Ask your strategists these questions:

a What is the timeline to maturity of the trends we have identified? Are these happening now; imminent; likely to impact us in less than a year; upcoming but not yet here; or way out on the horizon at an undefined time?

b What is the likelihood these new trends will actually come to fruition in the market? Is it certain, high, possible, or remote?

c What secondary impacts can you imagine? That is, can you combine two or more of these trends to create new value in unprecedented ways? If so, how?

d What are the key indicators we should watch to determine if a specific trend is going to impact our members?

4 *Act.*

Based on what you're learning, allocate some resources and send up trial balloons. Consider funding several projects like a venture capitalist would, with the idea that most will die, a few will tread water, and one or two will take off. Start pilots small enough that you can easily sustain the losses, or fund their success on the tiny margins they're likely to generate. When you experience a failure, take it apart to determine why it didn't take off. If you have a success, begin tweaking it for growth.

5 *Measure.*

Measure what you can, but don't confine your analysis to quantitative results. Every disruption begins with unintended consequences. Bring together players, customers, and strategists to think together and generate insights and discoveries that will enable your next prototype.

Just as we should never stop marketing, we can never stop learning about our customers and their emerging unmet needs. The best leaders have systems for making that learning happen. It all comes down to regularly engaging smart people, scanning the environment, connecting the dots, trying new things, and learning from both successes and failures.

For more, look for my upcoming book in this series, Strategic Foresight Playbook.

In other words—

W A S H .   R I N S E .   R E P E A T . . . .

Practice 3. Driving Digital Business

Customers have changed irrevocably. They expect you to anticipate their needs; to know more about them than ever before while simultaneously respecting their privacy. They expect you to engage in lightning-fast transactions 24/7 around the globe.

If you can't or won't, they move on without you. Even so, most associations have yet to establish the foundations of a digital business strategy or secure clean data to monitor and analyze the basics. And where they have, innovation is lacking.

This is the time to put your digital house in order. It's imperative.

Investing in technology has never been cheaper and the returns have never come faster. Organization leaders who want to remain at the top of their members' priorities assess their organization's capabilities while growing its skill in data analytics. Your leaders should actively investigate developments in artificial intelligence, blockchain, global Internet access, robotics, cybersecurity, facial recognition, nanotechnology, and other rapidly developing breakthroughs.

Rather than issuing top-down mandates and dedicating data governance to the CIO, ensure the entire senior management team plus key volunteers have access to your information and the ability to use it, developing and sharing the insights that lead to your growth.

Institute transparent systems that unleash the collective knowledge of star performers across the organization and enable cross-unit collaboration. Technology is pervasive as are the innovators who leverage it, so open up your shop.

Digital business is here. You must engage as if your organization's relevance depends on it—because it does.

Too many associations do a decent job of updating hardware and software, but never look at where the digital ecosystem needs to be disrupted and expanded to compete effectively in a new member environment. They methodically upgrade desktops, move servers to the cloud, and deploy new accounting or AMS systems. But they do it to perpetuate current systems in a more state-of-the-art manner. What I am driving at here is understanding the overall transformations taking place in your members' lives and combining applications to deliver new forms of value.

In my work helping associations to retool for the 21st century, we always incorporate digital business transformation. This includes:

- ✓ Assessing digital assets and digital talent.
- ✓ Envisioning full digital integration across all channels that convey value to members; i.e., describing in some detail what happens when digital integration delivers a good (or great) customer experience.
- ✓ Describing the value of digital integration across multiple functions including talent acquisition, leadership

development, internal communication, finance, marketing, business development, membership development, meetings, and governance.

✓ Creating a game plan for migrating to digital business that is appropriate to the organization's budget, size, and capabilities.

To do this well, an orientation is required because digital business is a fundamental and evolutionary step beyond business-as-usual for the last 100 years. Wrapping one's head around it requires time to learn, digest, and discuss implications. These implications include how digitization is impacting and will impact your association's sector as well as association operations.

We have now examined the first three of the *five practices that lead to real-time strategy* and their requirements:

1 *Dealing with Disruption* allows you to effectively identify emerging disruptions before they impact you, respond with threat assessments, and develop your ability to introduce disruptions into your market.

2 *Instituting Strategic Foresight* enables you to look farther and more deeply into the future, so you can avoid surprises where possible and prepare to leverage emerging trends for greater impact.

3 *Driving Digital Business* gives you the tools your members are coming to rely on and your competitors will use against you.

With these three practices internalized, the organization is ready to work on the last two practices: scaling for impact and creating new partnerships. This is the territory of the Grand Challenge.

A Grand Challenge is a *bold*,

socially beneficial initiative

that brings people, organizations,

and powerful resources

together

to solve intractable problems.

Four

THE GRAND CHALLENGE

"[C]ompanies that build scale for the benefit of their customers and shareholders more often succeed over time."

—Jamie Dimon, Chairman and CEO, JPMorgan Chase

Sometimes "grand challenge" is used to refer to the intractable problem itself, though it may also refer to a collective initiative designed to help solve it. A Grand Challenge is not a one-off program or even a strategic campaign; it relies on the creation of a social movement.

I have been fortunate to be involved with launching and developing some amazing Grand Challenge initiatives, including Healthy Nurse Healthy Nation™ by the American Nurses Association; the Thriving Earth Exchange by the American Geophysical Union; and the Center for Financial Planning by the CFP Board of Standards. Each of these has taken the specialized needs and knowledge of their sector and used it to create value that extends far beyond traditional stakeholders.

Through *Healthy Nurse Healthy Nation™*, the American Nurses Association seeks to improve the lives of America's 3.6 million registered nurses, their families, their communities, and the country. Its agenda is to "connect and engage nurses, employers, and organizations around improving health in five areas: physical activity, nutrition, rest, quality of life, and safety."[11]

The American Beverage Association's initiative outlined in the beginning of this book is an example of a Grand Challenge, uniting the major soda manu-

facturers to support family efforts to balance what their children eat, drink, and do including the reduction of sugar from beverages consumed at school. By year three of this initiative, the ABA and the major beverage companies had achieved a remarkable 88 percent reduction in beverage calories shipped to schools.

CFP Board of Standard's Grand Challenge, the Center for Financial Planning, has a clear mission: to "create a more diverse and sustainable financial planning profession." Through research, education, and workforce development, the Center for Financial Planning aims to directly increase the number of certified financial planners who are women and minorities.[12]

Grand Challengers use tools that imbue their mission with the powers of shared purpose, attracting conscious collaboration through collective leadership. They bring forward an unprecedented level of understanding and action to address a new scale of social impact. And they offer unique returns for all who participate.

A truly Grand Challenge will never be easy; some failure and struggle will happen. But the enthusiastic efforts of committed people to create large-scale change is possible. Breakthroughs in quantum physics tell us that the very act of observation changes what we observe. In this way, setting your sights on a Grand Challenge will impact what you perceive, opening possibilities for solutions to emerge around you.

A key characteristic of a Grand Challenge is that the partners who commit to realizing its goal work in their own ways to achieve success. They enroll their social networks and contribute their specialized knowledge and distinct skills. Their effort unfolds around the clock, multiplying force and leading to continuous impact; it's not limited to 9-5/Monday-Friday. Grand Challenges operate in real time to tackle big issues.

The primary tool for achieving them is the creation of a social movement. This means you'll want to develop new business processes for supporting and amplifying impact, as well as harvesting the value. An illustration can be seen in the effective use of social media.

While hosting a meeting of associations engaged in Grand Challenges, I convened a session on social media and brought in Heather Holdridge, the director of digital strategy for Planned Parenthood. The organization is an acknowledged leader in the use of social media to raise a lot of money or mobilize many votes quickly. I brought Holdridge in to study their methods. She described how Facebook and Twitter strengthened Planned Parenthood, which has seen itself in political crosshairs since 2011. According to her, we should all be so lucky as to have moments when issues important to us come into public consciousness.

It's much easier to ride a wave than create a wave. She laid out how Planned Parenthood rides the social media wave, even in turbulent waters, by sharing the following principles with me for a blog post in 2015. Whether or not you agree with their politics, Planned Parenthood's leaders are experts in creating results, so their strategy deserves our attention.

1 *To create a groundswell of support, till the soil.*

When Congress attempted to defund Planned Parenthood in 2011, we began to see Facebook posts and photos we didn't create. One image that became iconic is three people dressed as Storm Troopers holding a sign that reads: 'Stand with Planned Parenthood.' We realized our greatest asset was not our 700 health centers in 50 states; it was people who valued a relationship with Planned Parenthood. We let them know we appreciated their tweets and posts.

We have amplified what they do on our platforms and we now boost the visibility of their photos, personal stories, and messages. We established a standard hashtag, #StandwithPP. After the vote to defund us, that hashtag rocketed to the top of Twitter, surpassing even #nationalcheeseburgerday.

2 *Give up ownership.*

Support on social media is organic and authentic. You may create a hashtag but you don't own it. Let people run with it. Suggest ways supporters can channel their energy and show support. There is a lot of creativity and humor out there that can serve you.

Another independent group launched the Facebook page, 'Humans of Planned Parenthood.' It has become a very active community. We have no control over the content, but we acknowledge them.

3   *Diversify to focus messaging.*
    We originally had a single Facebook page and one Twitter
    handle. We realized we need to speak with two distinct
    voices. Some rely on us for health-related information and we
    needed to reach them with an encouraging, nonjudgmental
    voice. Another audience cares about our survival and
    women's access to healthcare. We use a sharper voice to
    express threats to the organization. Now we maintain more
    than one presence on Facebook and Twitter so we can focus
    our messaging and deliver it in a consistent tone.

4   *Anticipate emotion and steer the energy in a productive direction.*
    There are times when you get bushwhacked, as we did with
    the leaked videos in 2015. But there are other moments-in-
    the-making that allow you to prepare. Last year, we knew the
    Supreme Court ruling on the Hobby Lobby case was coming
    and that the outcome would probably be bad news for access
    to birth control. We prepared a graphic and template that
    allowed us to immediately distribute an email, highlighting
    Justice Ginsburg's blistering dissent.

5   *Remain vigilant and nimble.*
    This year, we were not as nimble in responding to the videos
    released by an anti-abortion group. We didn't see this well-
    orchestrated attack coming. It took several days to respond
    and give our supporters an explanation. People wanted to
    know what to do. We weren't ready with the answers they
    needed as quickly as we should have been.

    However, we typically are responsive because we don't
    have a rigorous approval process for social media. We work
    collaboratively with our Government Relations team to

identify messages we can optimize for social media. You cannot afford to let a review process slow you down.[13]

For many associations, these tactics for creation of a social movement are not business-as-usual. It requires advance preparation to be able to respond in real time without burdensome processes.

This brings us to the fourth practice of the five practices that lead to real-time strategy.

Practice 4. Scaling for Impact

Scalable impact takes you beyond incremental growth. It means you are leveraging the work you're doing today to get a multiple on the return. True business growth relies on scaling. If you put in more resources and get a corresponding ROI, you're not really growing. When you scale, you put in a little more resources and get a lot more growth.

Traditionally, association impact has been limited to members and their value network—a finite set. This approach artificially caps your impact. When you open up the benefits of your work to reach beyond your members' value networks, you can scale your impact dramatically.

Every association has this treasured asset: to leverage the experience and expertise of their members for the benefit of a much larger set of people. If your members are 65,000 earth and space scientists, for example, and you can leverage their discoveries for *all of humanity,* you have extended the beneficiaries from 68,000 to 7.6 billion. Your resources now reach almost 117,000 times as many people! *That's* scalable impact.

Identify all constituencies who have a stake in your success and discover resource opportunity writ large.

By demonstrating that your work benefits a much larger set of stakeholders, you place your organization in a position to identify additional funding, knowledge, and workers. You can extend beyond members and their value networks to reach others who benefit from your results. For instance, if you can fill a workforce pipeline that is declining, you're in a position to solicit funding and other forms of support from the organizations that benefit from the additional workers. As long as the investment they make in your organization is less than the value they receive, it's a good deal for everyone.

Associations that grow beyond the confines of tradition will master scalable impact and extend their unique value to much larger sets of beneficiaries. This is exactly what a *Grand Challenge* does.

Once you've identified a Grand Challenge that can take your association beyond incremental growth, the next step is to build your partnerships, which brings us to the final practice that leads to real-time strategy.

Practice 5

Building New Kinds of Partnerships

Associations have long had partners, but new forms are emerging that bring together players in novel constellations to work together on a common agenda. Many use the *fleet* as a metaphor, pulling together a handful of large organizations which provide power, cover, and presence along with smaller organizations that are nimble and capable of changing direction quickly to explore new developments for the path ahead.

Arising from the social sector, the *collective impact* method brings multiple organizations and activists together to work toward a common goal. This is the method I use when building a Grand Challenge. Below are some of its elements, along with guidelines for thinking about these new partnerships.

"If it can be solved by a single discipline, it isn't a Grand Challenge. And if it doesn't scare you, it's not grand enough!"

—Marla Weston, former CEO of the American Nurses Association

A truly systemic, intractable problem requires the joining together of multiple leaders from multiple organizations across multiple disciplines. Since the complexity of Grand Challenges requires shared leadership and fluid autonomy rather than hierarchical, command-and-control structures, no single organization will take the lead. However, a single association can serve as the *backbone organization*, providing coordination, communication, definition, and assessment of metrics, thus linking together disparate players in a unified play for a goal everyone is invested in achieving.

When the U.S. Army joined the American Nurses Association in support of Healthy Nurse, Healthy Nation™, they did so because lack of health among nurses constitutes a national security threat. The army sees ANA's initiative as an opportunity to ensure the readiness of their fighting forces. CVS Caremark joined the same initiative because they are committed to improving the health of the 9,000+ nurses on their payroll. Their *common agenda*—improving the health of nurses—was an end state all three organizations (and the many other partners who joined in) required to achieve their own goals. This is an example of how a unifying objective drives new partnerships working for collective impact.

Associations that develop new partnerships outside their traditional reach build more robust support for their goals and public image, allowing them to achieve new heights. Social movements form, bolstering and lifting the association and its partners together to greater levels of performance.

These are the five elements of real-time strategy: dealing with disruption; instituting strategic foresight; driving digital business; scaling for impact; and forming new kinds of partnerships. They represent the association of the 21st century: looking ahead; ready for tumult; digitally savvy; able to leverage member value for much larger stakeholder constituencies; and much more integrated with the world around it.

Collective Action to Do Good

I began this book with the example of Visonary Leader Susan Neely. To conclude the book, I return to the example of the American Beverage Association she led.

In 2006, the American Beverage Association (ABA) signed on to create large-scale change. Together with the Clinton Global Initiative, a major NGO, and powerful private sector collaboration, they agreed to help create industry change in the bottling, distribution, and sale of beverages at U.S. schools, changing the ingredients (e.g., reducing sugar), size, and calories of major soda and bottled juice brands.

Parents, teachers, and healthcare professionals had grown deeply concerned about the quality of the beverage products marketed to children and adolescents in American schools, though most didn't want to see the sale of these beverages entirely eradicated. Instead, they demanded change from the industry, and change is what they got.

Everyone in the country knew about the "cola wars"—major American soda brands were infamous for their fierce competition. And yet the cost of the multimillion-dollar undertaking was paid for by the companies themselves. Against what may have been their short-term financial best interests, Coke™, Pepsi™, and Dr. Pepper™ took the lead, aligning together in an unheard-of venture to alter their own products for the good of the consumer, rather than their own bottom lines.

Machines had to be refitted and valuable brand real estate on products themselves had to be sacrificed in order to make room for calorie labels, but the brands agreed to make the necessary changes in an effort Neely refers to as *Collective Action to Do Good.*

They were convinced to align because of the "existential threat" on their mutual horizon, says Neely. The country has begun trending toward health consciousness, and consumers are more aware and concerned than ever about what is in the products they consume. Americans are choosing to hold even major brands accountable for mounting public health concerns like obesity, and if the brands fail to respond with accountability and action, they will be left behind. Consider the sweeping culture change around smoking since the 1980s and its impact on Big Tobacco, which lost billions to court cases, plunging product sales, and changing public sentiment.

In the end, Neely says the ABA's work helped to see a 90 percent reduction in beverage calories shipped to American schools. As a result of its success, more and similar models for sweeping change were created.

Neely is convinced; when organizational leaders look ahead and see an existential threat bearing down on their industries, they must be willing to take a *for* position," rather than resting on business-as-usual instincts to align themselves against impending change.

The value ABA was able to contribute to society and the credibility their work brought to bear on the organization—to be effective on the part of their partner organizations—was greatly amplified as a result of their participation in this Grand Challenge. The results energized Neely's conviction and effectiveness as a leader. She no longer believes that what they and their partners did is right; she *knows* it is.

What's more, taking a *for* position on behalf of positive change for consumers made the organization more successful, not less. Collective Action to Do Good generates positive public regard and makes for more loyal members and customers. This goes well beyond corporate social responsibility campaigns; it is about *societal* responsibility and positive culture change.

In 2008, First Lady Michelle Obama announced her aim to launch a movement around ending childhood obesity. As soon as they heard the news, Susan Neely reached out to the White House, offering ABA's support toward the endeavor. The reply was a resounding, "yes." And in 2009 when Mrs. Obama formally announced the "Let's Move" initiative, ABA was the single food industry representative standing with her at the launch.

SETH KAHAN'S
VISIONARY
LEADERSHIP

Conclusion

In this book I have introduced my insights and recommendations concerning association strategy in the age of disruption. I have drawn on my consulting work with hundreds of association leaders who are coping with real-world challenges and opportunities, in real time. But the ultimate test of this material is its usefulness to you. Please send stories of your experiences as you apply these principles, and suggestions for improvement, to Seth@VisionaryLeadership.com.

APPENDIX

Visionary Leadership Assessment and Evaluation

I have developed an assessment from diagnostic comparisons across my clients and body of work. It can be found here along with the evaluation notes, and on my website at **VisionaryLeadership.com/thebook.** You have my permission to copy or download this assessment and distribute it. I encourage you to take the assessment and create an executive action plan to develop your visionary leadership skills.

I have also found this assessment to provide excellent guidance for the Board of Directors and the executive team. I suggest you use this as an exercise at your next retreat, handing out the assessment and the evaluation. After everyone has completed it, you may go through the competencies to discuss your team's areas of strength and weakness.

You may also send me your board's or your executive team's assessment results and I will provide an interpretation of their results. Email them to Seth@VisionaryLeadership.com.

Complete this short assessment to find out

STRONGLY DISAGREE   1 — 2 — 3 — 4 — 5   STRONGLY AGREE

I. Personal Power

I make it a priority to...

_____ Purposefully do things I have never done before to add to my experience

_____ Use stories to get and hold people's attention on important topics

_____ Regularly make time for activities that renew and revitalize me

_____ Find innovative ways to package experience into stories that illustrate key lessons

_____ Ask members and staff about their life experience

_____ Listen for stories from members that hold valuable lessons

_____ Put myself in the shoes of people I don't agree with

_____ Guard my time that is scheduled for taking care of myself

_____ ADD THE NUMBERS ABOVE FOR YOUR TOTAL SCORE ON PERSONAL POWER

II. Association Leadership

I make it a priority to...

_____ Maintain an attitude of opportunism when circumstances are challenging

_____ Reach out to other parts of the organization to get insight

_____ Help others learn and grow in the face of adversity

_____ Find the silver lining in every major problem I encounter

_____ Find ways to join forces with other organizations to achieve our shared goals

New competencies in three categories—*Personal Power, Association Leadership, and Market Acumen*—prepare you for more effective collaboration with and influence on the systems in which you operate. I have developed this assessment to help you determine the areas that would most benefit your personal and professional growth.

____ Bring together multiple constituencies to address difficult issues
____ Excel at building partnerships across multiple organizations
____ Find alignment among parties who represent differing perspectives

____ ADD THE NUMBERS ABOVE FOR YOUR TOTAL SCORE ON ASSOCIATION LEADERSHIP

III. Market Acumen

I make it a priority to...

____ Read outside our association to understand how the world is changing.
____ Identify market changes that could have major impact on my association
____ Hunt for social trends that could threaten my association
____ Determine the disruptions that are likely to last
____ Educate myself on complicated trends
____ Dig deep and probe into new advances that impact our work
____ Contact our members and learn what is changing in their day-to-day work
____ Shift organizational priorities with the market, not waiting for periodic strategic planning

____ ADD THE NUMBERS ABOVE FOR YOUR TOTAL SCORE ON MARKET ACUMEN

Assessment Evaluation

Personal Power ────────────⟶ (── TOTAL SCORE)

16 or below: Your development is limiting your performance and your organization's potential. It is time to make your personal power a priority. Raise your game by getting involved in activities that stretch your self-development well beyond your comfort zone.

17 to 31: You have some skill when it comes to personal power but will still benefit by getting out of your comfort zone. Make some new friends who are creating results well beyond your own and enroll in an adventure that stretches your limits.

32 and above: You a high-performing leader. By taking your development seriously, you are investing in your ability to create extraordinary results. You have the leadership firepower it takes to be a visionary and follow it up with action.

Association Leadership ──────────⟶ (── TOTAL SCORE)

16 or below: Your leadership style is stale and generates equally stale organizational outcomes. Invest in yourself. Take a leadership course in which over half the participants are better leaders than you. Seek out peers who are doing better than you at creating exceptional results and learn from them.

17 to 31: You have solid skills but are still short on the visionary scale. It's time for you to take on a project that is so ambitious it intimidates you. Surround yourself with partners, colleagues, and leaders who have consistently generated bigger, bolder results than you have. Step up. Build your capacity to lead.

32 and above: You are a visionary leader for your association. You have positioned yourself and your organization to lead with exceptional results. Mentor others.

Market Acumen ⟶ (___ TOTAL SCORE)

16 or below: You are out of touch with today's market and your organization is vulnerable as a result. Dedicate time to studying the market: including members, potential members, partners, and competitors. Identify the trends most likely to upset your association's value proposition. Study how to increase the impact of your mission using new tools and techniques that have been developed in the last two years. Push yourself harder to understanding the market and how it influences your success.

17 to 31: You have some skill at understanding the market environment, but you could do better. Raise the bar. Dig deeper into the news. Identify thought leaders and reach out to them personally. Involve yourself in conversations with movers and shakers. Listen more than you speak. Ask close friends how you can up your game.

32 and above: You are a market maven. Share your knowledge and expertise with colleagues. Increase the leaders you are mentoring. Develop your ability to execute. Perfect your market moves.

Acknowledgements

Many people contributed to the invisible groundwork that made this book possible. In particular I am indebted to my clients who have worked with me on Grand Challenges:

- Ellen Bergfeld, Alliance of Crop, Soil and Environmental Science Societies
- Dale Cyr, Inteleos
- Kevin Keller & Marilyn Mohrman-Gillis, the Center for Financial Planning
- Chris McEntee, the Thriving Earth Exchange powered by AGU
- Marla Weston, the American Nurses Association Enterprise

In addition, these Grand Challenge leaders have been generous to me with their time and perspectives:

- Susan Neely, American Council of Life Insurers
- Michelle Popowitz & Jill Sweitzer Redell, UCLA Department of Grand Challenges

Julie Jordan Avritt, writer, co-creator, and alchemist has not only contributed but infused me with enthusiasm over and over again for elucidating the visionary.

For her writing and book craft, Sarah White.

I am indebted to these special leaders who read the book pre-publication and furnished valuable input, much of which is reflected in this text:

- Dale Cyr, Inteleos
- Mark Golden, National Society of Professional Engineers
- Gary Labranche, National Investor Relations Institute

I am especially thankful for my wife's support. Laura Baron has been an inspiration with her music and soul sustenance. In particular, her song, **Kindness Don't Rest Easy**, which you can hear at LauraBaronMusic.com!

Cheers to each of you! I raise a glass of bubbly in gratitude. Let's see, that's a good fourteen glasses now...

Notes

1   Christensen, Clayton, "Disruptive Innovation Explained,"
    Filmed March 2012. YouTube video, 7:51. Posted March 2012—
    www.youtu.be/qDrMAzCHFUU

2   October 11, 2017, the New York Times reported BlackRock's
    total assets to be $5.9 trillion. www.nyti.ms/2kHqOsD

3   Kaku, Michio, *Physics of the Future: How Science Will Shape
    Human Destiny and Our Daily Lives by the Year 2100*, (New York:
    Doubleday 2011), 7.

4   www.kurzweilai.net/the-law-of-accelerating-returns

5   My good friend and mindfulness buddy, Rob Creekmore, was
    fond of saying this to me on many of our long walks together.

6   Denning, Stephen, *The Springboard: How Storytelling Ignites
    Action in Knowledge-Era Organizations, Routledge*; 1st edition
    (November 24, 2015)

7   www.diamandis.com/blog/problems-are-goldmines

8   www.ssir.org/articles/entry/collective_impact

9   www.yellowstonepark.com/things-to-do/
    wolf-reintroduction-changes-ecosystem

10 www2.deloitte.com/content/dam/insights/us/articles
    /3407_2016-Shift-Index/DUP_2016-Shift-Index.pdf

11 www.healthynursehealthynation.org

12 www.centerforfinancialplanning.org/about-the-center/
    mission-and-vision

13 Seth Kahan, "Social Media for National Movement," Visionary
    Leadership Blog, December 6, 2015.
    www.visionaryleadership.com/carpe-momentum-
    social-media-for-national-movement

Index

About the Author

Seth Kahan is an executive strategist. He is a recognized expert on innovation and specializes in association leadership. He has served over 100 association CEOs, worked closely with the president of the World Bank, served the director of the Peace Corps; and assisted senior managers at Royal Dutch Shell, Prudential Retirement, and Abt Associates.

Seth provides strategic planning, board development, senior team development, and works closely with CEOs on the design and execution of their Grand Challenges.

He has earned the designation of Thought-leader and Exemplar in Change Leadership from the Society for Advancement of Consulting® and the title of Visionary from the Center for Association Leadership. He served as a director on the boards of the American Geophysical Union, the Columbia Lighthouse for the Blind, the Council of Better Business Bureaus, and the Wood Acres Citizens Association.

Seth is the author of the business bestseller, *Getting Change Right: How Leaders Transform Organizations from the Inside Out*, *Getting Innovation Right: How Leaders Leverage Inflection Points to Drive Success*, and *Building Beehives: A Handbook for Creating Communities that Generate Returns*.

He publishes a weekly newsletter, *Monday Morning Mojo*, and a weekly video blog, *Visionary Talk*. You can subscribe to either at VisionaryTalk.com.

CONTACT SETH DIRECTLY AT SETH@VISIONARYLEADERSHIP.COM

WWW.VISIONARYLEADERSHIP.COM